Wireless Networks

Series Editor
Xuemin Sherman Shen
University of Waterloo
Waterloo, Ontario, Canada

More information about this series at http://www.springer.com/series/14180

Deze Zeng • Lin Gu • Song Guo

Cloud Networking
for Big Data

Springer

Deze Zeng
China University of Geosciences
Wuhan, Hubei, China

Song Guo
School of Computer Science
    and Engineering
The University of Aizu
Aizu-Wakamatsu City, Japan

Lin Gu
Huazhong University of Science and Tech
Wuhan, Hubei, China

ISSN 2366-1186   ISSN 2366-1445   (electronic)
Wireless Networks
ISBN 978-3-319-24718-2   ISBN 978-3-319-24720-5   (eBook)
DOI 10.1007/978-3-319-24720-5

Library of Congress Control Number: 2015952315

Springer Cham Heidelberg New York Dordrecht London

Springer International Publishing AG Switzerland is part of Springer Science+Business Media (www.
springer.com)

Preface

The explosive growth of big data imposes a heavy burden on computation, storage, and communication resources in today's infrastructure. To efficiently exploit the bulk cloud resources for big data processing, many different parallel cloud computing programming frameworks, such as Apache Hadoop, Spark, and Twitter Storm, have been proposed and widely applied. However, all these programming paradigms mainly focus on data storage and computation, while still treating the communication issue as blackbox. How data are transmitted in the network is transparent to the application developers. Although such paradigm makes application development easy, an increasing concern to manipulate the data transmission in the network according to the application requirements emerges and asks for flexible, customizable, secure, and efficient networking control. The gap between the computation programming and communication programming shall be filled up. Fortunately, the recent development in some newly emerging technologies such as software-defined networking (SDN) and network function virtualization (NFV) stimulates cloud networking innovation towards big data processing. We are motivated to present the concept of cloud networking for big data in this monograph.

Based on the understanding of cloud networking technology, we further present two case studies to provide high-level insights on how cloud networking technology can benefit big data application on the perspective of cost-efficiency. With the rising number of data centers all over the world, the electricity consumption and communication cost have been increasing drastically as the main operational expenditure (OPEX) to data centers. Therefore, cost minimization has become an emergent issue for data centers in big data era. Different from conventional cloud services, one of the main features of big data services is the tight coupling between data and computation as computation tasks can be conducted only when the corresponding data is available. As a result, three factors, i.e., task assignment, data placement, and data movement, deeply influence OPEX of geo-distributed data centers. Thanks to cloud networking, we are able to pursue cost minimization via joint optimization of these three factors for big data applications in geo-distributed data centers. We first characterize the data processing procedure using a two-dimensional Markov chain and derive the expected completion time in closed-form, based on which the joint optimization is formulated as a mixed-integer nonlinear programming (MINLP) problem. To tackle the high computational complexity of solving our MINLP, we linearize it into a mixed-integer linear programming (MILP) problem. Experiment results show that our joint-optimization solution has substantial advantage over the approach by two-step separate optimization.

We further notice that processing large numbers of continuous data streams, i.e., big data stream processing (BDSP), has become a crucial requirement for many scientific and industrial applications in recent years. Public cloud service providers usually operate a number of geo-distributed data centers across the globe. Different data center pairs are with different inter-data center network costs due to the different locations and distances. While inter-data center traffic in BDSP constitutes a large portion of a cloud provider's traffic demand over the Internet and incurs substantial communication cost, which may even become the dominant OPEX factor. As the data center resources are provided in a virtualized way, the virtual machines (VMs) for stream processing tasks can be freely deployed onto any data centers, provided that the service level agreement (SLA, e.g., quality-of-information) is obeyed. This raises the opportunity, but also a challenge, to explore the inter-data center network cost diversity to optimize both VM placement and load balancing towards network cost minimization with guaranteed quality-of-information. Fortunately, cloud networking makes such optimization possible. We first propose a general modeling framework that can transform the VM placement into VM selection problem and describe all representative inter-task relationship semantics in BDSP. Based on our novel framework, we then formulate the communication cost minimization problem for BDSP into a MILP problem and prove it to be NP-hard. We then propose a computation-efficient solution based on MILP. The high efficiency of our proposal is also validated by extensive simulation-based studies.

Keywords: Cloud networking, Software-defined networking, Network function virtualization, Cloud computing, Geo-distributed data centers, Cost efficiency, Big data, Resource management and optimization.

Waterloo, ON, Canada   Xuemin Sherman Shen
Wuhan, Hubei, China   Deze Zeng
Wuhan, Hubei, China   Lin Gu
Aizu-Wakamatsu City, Japan   Song Guo

Acknowledgements

We first would like to express our heartfelt gratitude to Dr. Xuemin (Sherman) Shen, who reviewed and offered professional and constructive comments to improve this monograph. We are equally grateful to Susan Lagerstrom-Fife and Jennifer Malat who provided support in the process of editing. Without their generous help, this monograph would have been hardly possible. We also would like to thank all the readers who are interested in this newly emerging area and our monograph. Last but not least: I beg forgiveness of all those who have helped a lot and whose names I have failed to mention.

Contents

Acronyms

ARPANet	Advanced Research Project Agency Network
AWS	Amazon Web Service
BDBP	Big Data Batch Processing
BDSP	Big Data Stream Processing
BSP	Backward Speculative Placement
CAPEX	Capital Expenditure
CBD	Cut-Based Decomposition
DARD	Distributed Adaptive Routing for Data Centers
DC	Data Center
DCR	Data Center Resizing
DNS	Domain Name Service
DPI	Deep Packet Inspection
EMS	Element Management System
HDFS	Hadoop Distributed File System
IaaS	Infrastructure as a Service
ILP	Integer Linear Programming
JVM	Java Virtual Machine
MILP	Mixed-integer Linear Programming
MINLP	Mixed-integer Nonlinear Programming
NaaS	Network as a Service
NAT	Network Address Translation
NBI	Northbound Interface
NCP	Network Control Program
NF	Network Function
NFV	Network Function Virtualization
NFVI	Network Function Virtualization Infrastructure
NPI	Network programming Interface
NSFNet	National Science Foundation Network
ONF	Open Networking Foundation
OPEX	Operational Expenditure
PaaS	Platform as a Service

PBD	Pivot Bit Decomposition
PM	Physical Machine
QoS	Quality of Service
SaaS	Software as a Service
SBI	Southbound Interface
SDN	Software Defined Networking or Software Defined Network
SLA	Service Level Agreement
TCAM	Ternary Content Addressable Memory
TCP	Transmission Control Program
VM	Virtual Machine
VNF	Virtualized Network Function
VoD	Video-on-Demand
WWW	World Wide Web

Part I
Network Evolution Towards Cloud Networking

Chapter 1
Background Introduction

Like any other technology, cloud networking is a natural evolution due to the technology development and requirement stimulation. In this chapter, let us first briefly review the networking history to understand how it evolves to cloud networking. We then introduce cloud computing and big data as its enabling technology and driving force, respectively.

1.1 Networking Evolution

Computer networking traces its beginnings back to 1960s. It is widely agreed that today's global Internet started from the Advanced Research Projects Agency Network (ARPANet) of the U.S. Department of Defense in 1969, based on the concept published in 1967. Initially, it has only 4 official nodes at UCLA (University of California, Los Angeles), Standford Research Institute (SRI), UCSB (University of California, Santa Barbara), and the University of Utah. The initial purpose of ARPANet was to share computer resources among scientists in these four connected institutions. The concept of packet as information transmission unit that is able to be routed on different paths and reconstructed at the intended destination was invented then. Accordingly, Network Control Program (NCP) [1] was introduced as a symmetric computer-to-computer networking protocol for network participation, data flow routing, host addressing. Thanks to NCP, the world's first node-to-node message was successful sent from UCLA to SRI and more nodes were able to join the network. The number of hosts was increased to 15 in 1971. ARPANet even become international in 1973 with the involvement of the University of London and Norway's Royal Radar Establishment.

In 1970s, the construction of ARPANet stimulated the development of many new networking technologies. For example, in 1974, Ethernet allowing intra-connection within Xerox company (i.e., local area networks) was created and demonstrated by

© Springer International Publishing Switzerland 2015
D. Zeng et al., *Cloud Networking for Big Data*, Wireless Networks,
DOI 10.1007/978-3-319-24720-5_1

Robert Metcalfe and David Boggs, who were therefore listed as Ethernet inventors in the patent application. In the same year, Vinton Cerf and Robert Kahn, who later were recognized as "the fathers of the Internet," published "A Protocol for Packet Network Interconnection" [2] and engaged in the development of Transmission Control Program (TCP) to incorporate both connection-oriented and datagram transmission services. This protocol later replaced NCP and became the standard for ARPANet. On January 1st, 1983, NCP was officially abandoned and eventually replaced by TCP/IP in the ARPANET, marking the start of the modern Internet [3]. With the adoption of Ethernet and TCP/IP protocol, data transmission in network became more quickly and efficiently. The network size also increased. It was reported that the total number of connected computers in ARPANet increased to 1000 by 1984. With the development and incorporation of personal computer (PC), the total number of network hosts broke 10,000 by 1987 and the number was suddenly ten timed to reach 100,000 by 1989.

In contrary to the openness of TCP/IP, the government funded background made ARPANet only available to authorized enterprises and research agencies. Individual unauthorized users were excluded from ARPANet. This more or less constrained the development and popularity of ARPANet. To deal with the ever-growing demands for public data communication services, a wide-area network, National Science Foundation Network (NSFNet), replaced ARPANet as the backbone network for connecting universities and research facilities in 1991 and finally developed into a major part of the Internet backbone. The year of 1991 is also regarded as the flag year of World Wide Web (WWW) as Tim Berners-Lee developed and released it in this year. WWW is an information system of interlinked hypertext documents that are accessible through the Internet. Since then, the development of Internet and WWW was ignited. In 1994, the WWW burst all over the world with an annual growth of 341,634 % [4]. The success of WWW also drove the development of Internet as the latter performs as the communication backbone to support the former.

Today's Internet is populated with several billions of hosts worldwide. According to a recent survey, around 40 % of the world population enjoy the Internet connection in 2013 while the number was less than 1 % in 1995 [5]. Figure 1.1 shows the growth of global Internet users since 1993. We can see that the number of Internet users has increased more than tenfold since 1993 by 2014.

What is astonishing is that the TCP/IP protocol suite initially designed for only few connected devices still functions well in today's large-scale Internet. This is attributed to the simpleness, distribution, and blackbox design principles of TCP/IP. Simpleness means that the protocol suite only provides the functions of transmitting and routing between hosts while all other intelligences are put in the hosts. Distribution indicates that there is no central network administration or control. The whole network operates in a distributive, self-learning, and self-management manner. Blackbox design principle refers to that the internal changes and operations are standardized and invisible. Programmers do not need to concern the details in the underlying network behaviors. But in this case, programmers also do not have the privilege to control the network even if there are such demands.

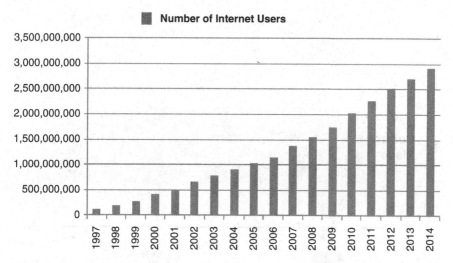

Fig. 1.1 Number of Internet users

The success of Internet practically proves that TCP/IP is really a brilliant design. However, with the recent development of information and communication technologies, the limitations and shortcomings of this general one-fit-all TCP/IP solution are increasingly exposed. Different applications may have different demands and highly dynamic communication, consequently requiring different networking resources. Current network devices lack the flexibility to deal with different application needs because of the underlying hardwired implementation of routing rules [6]. It is also hugely labor-intensive to reprogrammed traditional network devices [7, 8]. It is an obvious and urgent need that further amendment to enable dynamic, flexible, customizable, cost-effective, and adaptive networking paradigm must be made. This raises the proposal of Software-Defined Networking (SDN) technology (Fig. 1.2).

In contrast to the distributed management of traditional network architecture, SDN provides a centralized management and controlling of network services through an abstraction of the hardware-level functionalities via decoupling data plane from control plane. By such means, it is able to control the behaviors of entire network through a software program, enabling network administrators to build highly scalable, flexible, and adaptive networks, according to the data transmission needs. Data plane is mainly in charge of the data flow delivery between communication end hosts while control plane refers to the logical controller integrated with both network and service controller components responsible for network and service management. Control plane also provides APIs to allow application developers and network administrators to easily customize the network (e.g., routing rule, flow priority settings, topology control, etc.) and manage the services (e.g., service replica creation, load balancing, etc.). Programmers do not need to replace or reprogram hardware components in the core network. To achieve such vision, OpenFlow is proposed as a standardized protocol with strong industry

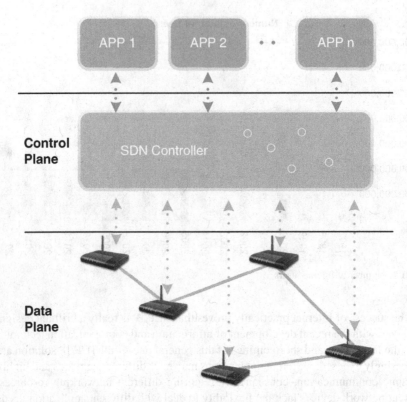

Fig. 1.2 Concept of SDN

support to ensure the secure and effective communication between control plane and data plane. The importance of SDN also urged the establishment of Open Networking Foundation (ONF) [9] in 2011 as a non-profit industry consortium to promote and standardize SDN and OpenFlow.

Today's computer networks consist of a large and growing variety of proprietary dedicated hardware devices while the hardware life cycle is becoming shorter and shorter due to the technology development and service innovation acceleration requirements. Meanwhile, to launch new networking services usually requires re-designing the underlying hardware or even new hardware purchasing. The variety of user demands makes it necessary to design, integrate, and operate increasingly complex hardware-based appliances, bringing increasing capital expenditure (CAPEX) and OPEX to our network-centric connected world.

Network Function Virtualization (NFV) is proposed to address this problem by leveraging present standard IT virtualization technology to consolidate various network equipment types onto virtualized standard high volume servers, switches and storage in data centers, network nodes and end hosts, as shown in Fig. 1.3. NFV virtualizes the network services such as network address translation (NAT), firewall, intrusion detection, and domain name service (DNS), which are presently carried

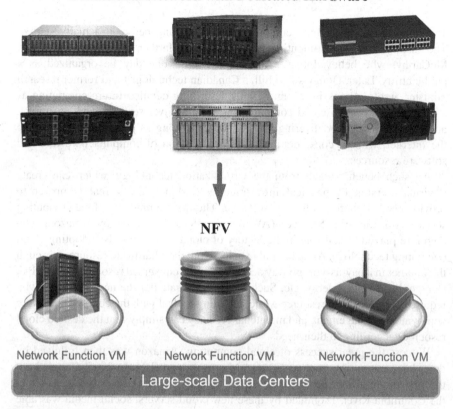

Fig. 1.3 Concept of NFV

out by proprietary and dedicated hardware. NFV aims to significantly reduce the amount of proprietary hardware needed to implement and operate network services. To approach this goal, NFV decouples network functions from dedicated hardware devices and virtualizes network functions carried out by dedicated hardware devices such as routers and firewalls to be hosted on virtual machines (VMs). All these network functions then can be performed on standard servers under the control of a hyper-visor without traditional dedicated hardware devices. In other words, NFV enables the possibility to leverage low-cost industry-standard commodity hardware, e.g., X86 servers, with independently developed networking software. Instead of managing and maintaining various complex hardware devices, network administrators now only need to simply deploy and schedule the network function VMs onto uniformed standard servers using NFV technology. Moreover, implementation of network functions in VMs running on standard servers can be moved to, or merged in, various locations in the network as required without purchasing new hardware devices.

1.2   Cloud Computing

The initial concept of cloud computing appeared long before it actually started. The history of cloud computing goes back even farther than 1960 with John McCarthy, who believed that computation should one day be organized as a public utility. Later, Douglas Parkhill, a Canadian technologist and former research minister, wrote a book in the mid-1960s describing detailed future computing as a utility. As expected, cloud computing now can deliver services such as storage and computation like delivering gas and water as long as users are connected to the Internet, without consideration of the localization of computer hardware and software resources.

All such benefits result from the virtualization technology, which can create a virtual version of physical infrastructures and act like a real computer to provide needed platforms for any software. The first commercial cloud computing service Amazon Web Services (AWS) was released in 2006 by Amazon, who therefore played a vital role in the history of cloud computing. By adopting cloud computing technology, Amazon is able to lease out their hardware resources through the Internet in a pay-as-you-go way according to the consumed resources, e.g., CPU, storage, bandwidth, energy, etc. Such idea exactly satisfies the needs of users who require a large scalable resource while unwilling to deal with the complex hardware deployment, management, and maintenance. They can simply rent the desired cloud resources according to their needs.

Witness the great success of cloud computing, Amazon was then followed by other large enterprises such as Google, Microsoft, and IBM. In 2005, Google built the first modern data center on 30 acres of land in the Dalles of Oregon along the Columbia River. Promoted by these new cloud servers, social media was able to boom afterwards and delivered cloud computing services to more and more people as is seen today. To support all cloud services above, large-scale data centers have been constructed all over the world. Nowadays as shown in Fig. 1.4, many enterprises as infrastructure providers have all released various cloud computing services supported by large-scale data centers to the public. These data centers are usually deployed in a geographically distributed manner. By now, Google already has 36 data centers across the globe. With 150 racks per data center, Google has more than 200,000 servers, running 24 h a day, 7 days a week [10]. Service providers, including both third-party companies who rent the cloud resources and those who own their own data centers, provide users with various services such as consulting, education, communications, storage, and processing. For reliability, security and expenditure benefits, more and more end users, both individuals and organizations, are moving their data and services from local to Internet data centers. To meet different requirements from users, cloud computing providers offer their services mainly in the following three paradigms. Their relationship is illustrated in Fig. 1.5.

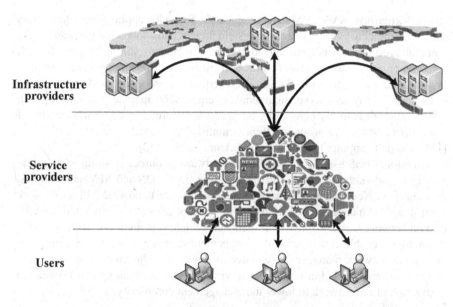

Infrastructure providers

Service providers

Users

Fig. 1.4 Cloud computing

Fig. 1.5 Cloud service paradigms

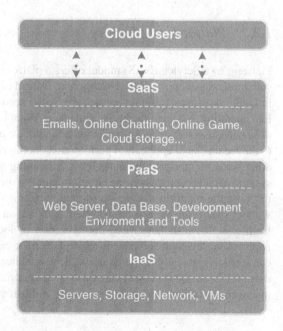

1.2.1 Infrastructure as a Service

Typical cloud providers of Infrastructure as a Service (IaaS) offer hardware resources in the form of VMs. The VMs run as guests by a hyper-visor, e.g., Xen,

Oracle VirtualBox, KVM, VMware, or Hyper-V. To deploy applications, cloud users can install their customized operating system images and application software on the rent cloud resources. Since virtualized resources in IaaS are still in their raw format, e.g., computation, storage, bandwidth, users still need to maintain their operating systems and the application softwares. Nevertheless, users are freed from tedious tasks such as physical server maintenance, equipment upgrade, machine retrofit, and so on. IaaS is utility computing basis that users are charged by the amount of resources allocated or consumed. Representative IaaS services include IBM Cloud [11], Google Computer Engine [12], and Amazon EC2 [13].

Traditional IaaS usually only includes hardware resources as storage, computation, and bandwidth. Recently, with the development of SDN and NFV technologies, the concept of **Network as a Service (NaaS)** is proposed to provide API for network controlling and management. It is appealing concept to users since it can reduce the cost on network hardware such as routers and switches. In addition, SDN and NFV technologies enable elastic network management from any place at any time. This makes the network management as easy as we used to manage the computation and storage resources. Furthermore, the virtualization technology can provide an abstraction of the network to lower the management complexity.

1.2.2 Platform as a Service

Platform as a Service (PaaS) model offers a platform including basic hardware and software tools of application development, instead of only bare virtual resources like in IaaS. For example, in IaaS model, users still need to deploy all development tool like operating systems, databases, and so on. What is more, to guarantee the quality of service, users also need to maintain and allocate all of these resources according to the feedbacks of application performance monitoring tools. PaaS provider, on the other hand, supports all the underlying computing and software, such as operating system, database, programming environment, and web server. Users only need to log in to use the platform to develop or deploy their applications through an interface, without specifying the operating system and hardware requirement. This frees users from complex installation and configuration of local hardware and software for application development because the platform's computer and storage resources can scale dynamically to match users' demands, instead of manual allocation. PaaS users thus can run their softwares using this platform without worrying about the management of both underlying hardware and software layers.

1.2.3 Software as a Service

Software as a Service (SaaS) describes on-demand cloud software services which are provided to users through the Internet. Traditional software applications require users to first purchase and then install them onto local computers. Another problem in this manner is that the number of users and locations of software installation are limited. Specially for organization users, to deploy a software for all employees could lead to a considerable cost. Worse, after installation, users still need to worry about the updates and patches. Fortunately, in SaaS model, users, both individuals and organizations, are able to rent or access cloud software applications which are hosted in remote data centers, rather than buying and installing them on local PC. Typical SaaS services, like Google search, Dropbox, and Facebook, can be accessed via any Internet connected devices. There is no strong requirement on resources. The device could be a PC, laptop, or smart phones. Cloud applications outperform traditional ones in their scalability achieved by cloning tasks onto multiple VMs in various locations to meet dynamic work demands. For example, we can use Google search in any place by connecting to any local data center of Google. Moreover, applications are used online with files saved in the cloud rather than on individual local servers. This also frees the users from buying storage devices. Representative cloud storage services include DropBox [14], iCloud [15], and GoogleDrive [16]. Different software applications are provided online for a wide range of needs, including computing, tracking sales, performance monitoring, analysis, decision making, and communication. Similar to other cloud based services, the price of SaaS applications is typically charged monthly or yearly, scalable and adjustable for users to add in or cancel at any time.

1.3 Big Data

Today, there are approximately 1.5 trillion devices in the world (including PCs, TVs, tablets, smart phones, etc) and most of them are connected, and are continuously generating data, to the Internet. Cisco expects a 25 % increasement in connectivity every year and that means we can expect 50 billion connected devices by 2020 with 50 % connections booming during 2018–2020, as shown in Fig. 1.6. According to IBM, the growing connectivity to the Internet has led to 90 % of the total data in the world created in the last 2 years [17]. IDC predicts the number will reach 40 Zettabytes (ZB, 2^{70}B) by the year of 2020, 50 times the amount of information and 75 times the number of information containers of today [18], as shown in Fig. 1.7. Without doubt that we have entered the "big data" era. It can be envisioned that with the increasing number of connected devices, the amount of new created data will continue to skyrocket.

Big data is famous for its 3V characteristics:

- Volume: Big data includes large volume of data from billions of devices and users.
- Variety: Large amount of data are loose-structured and distributed with inter-connections and sequences between them.
- Velocity: Data usually involves time-stamped events. Certain data must be processed within a delay constraint; otherwise, they will vanish into thin air.

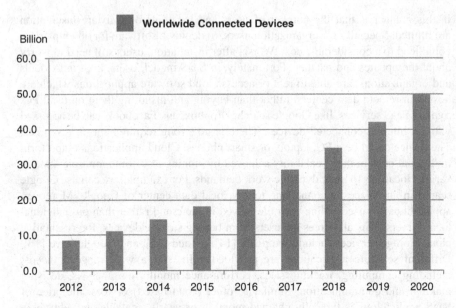

Fig. 1.6 Number of connected devices

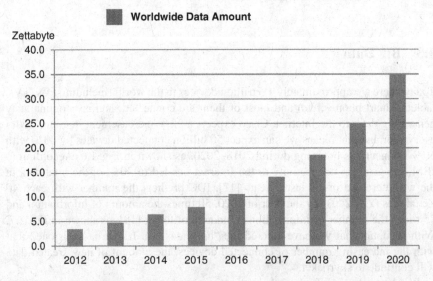

Fig. 1.7 Globe data amount

These characteristics make big data processing as a challenging task and raises many interests in both academia and industry. Big data solutions have tremendous momentum, and they are rapidly gaining more. Big data is making an increasing impact on academic world and moving into industry including IT campaniles, large chain stores, and wall street. The reason is clear. Big data delivers the opportunity to create positive changes. Generally, big data processing can be classified into two types of methods in terms of required processing latency. One is pre-stored batch processing and the other is real time stream processing.

1.3.1   Big Data Batch Processing

Batch processing has been associated with earliest mainframe computers since 1950s. There were a variety of reasons why batch processing dominated early computing. Firstly, the data volume back to then was small and computers were mainly used by large companies to do primarily accounting problems such as billing, which is a typical batch processing. Secondly, computing resources were expensive and the processing ability of computers was limited at that time. So sequential processing of batch jobs was a good choice for the resource constraints at the time. Even today, with powerful personal computers, smart phones and large-scale data centers, batch processing such as page ranking and credit card billing is still pervasive, especially with the recent emerging of big data. One representative example of big data batch processing is credit card billing. The customer does not receive a bill for each separate credit card purchase but one monthly bill for all of that month's purchases.

An overview of batch processing system, including three major components, is presented in Fig. 1.8. One input component in charge of collecting data from one or more sources, usually databases; a processing component performs computations using these inputs; and an output component generates results to be written back to databases.

In batch processing, the data are pre-stored in databases. In credit card billing, before actually processing the bills, all the related data must be collected and held until the bill is processed as a batch at the end of each month.

Fig. 1.8 Batch processing

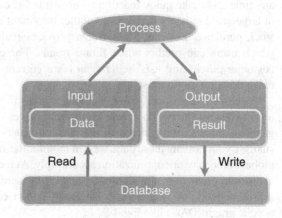

The performance of batch processing can be optimized by scheduling the sequences of job use different priorities, so users can keep a high overall utilization of computing resources. The simplicity of batch system also allows parallel processing, e.g., Hadoop. Rather than running one program multiple times, Hadoop runs the program once in many computation units, significantly reducing processing latency.

1.3.2 Big Data Stream Processing

In today's world, computing resources are comparatively cheap and cloud services are available around the clock. As a result, the delay expectation of users is significantly reduced. Many tasks shall be completed instantly like stock data analysis, immediate action shall be taken based on analysis results. This forces the concept of big data stream processing. We are generating an estimated 2.5 quintillion bytes of new information every day. To gain the greatest value from big data, data should be processed as soon as they arrive meanwhile data quality should also be maintained. That is to say, we have to process huge volumes of data fast enough to produce real time strategies for the largest competitive advantages. The biggest challenge is how to leverage available resources to handle such huge data volumes effectively. Imagine a continuous stream with new data arrives in 24 h a day, 7 days a week. We need to capture, process, and turn these data into immediate actions as soon as possible. It is obvious that traditional batch processing techniques are not suitable for stream data processing. The new technology shall allow the collection, integration, analysis of stream data, all in real time, without disrupting the activities in data sources, storage, and user systems.

Effective stream processing can solve a wide variety of real-world problems. For example, stream can be utilized as an online solution for fraud detection. As stream data are produced and received, system administrator can observe system status at any time and make quick reaction when a fraud is detected. This is very important in large-scale industry networks. Another important usage is decision making, e.g., stock purchase decision. Stream data provides real time system status based on which users can predict some future trends. For example, by cross-referencing customer purchasing lists, sellers can learn current customer buying patterns and make decision on future stock.

A sensor stream processing example is shown in Fig. 1.9. In this example, we have two sensor networks locate in different places of one area. Both continuously generate data streams including various information, e.g., sensing data, sensor status. By processing these data, we can monitor the status of all sensors and conduct globe online network optimization accordingly. At the same time, we can implement a disaster prediction application by analyzing sensing data streams from either sensor network. A stream processing application can be described as a directed acyclic graph (DAG) like Fig. 1.9.

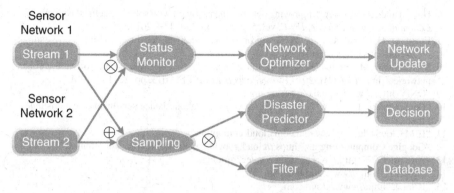

Fig. 1.9 Sensing data stream processing

Batch and stream data processing both have their advantages and disadvantages. How to select the best data processing system for a specific job depends on the types and sources of data, processing time requirements. There is a big demand for obtaining knowledge/regularity from the big data to create business values or make daily life more convenient and efficient. To store and process this large amount of data has become a heavy burden to service providers. Big data brings us big advantages along with big challenges.

1.4 Summary

In this chapter, we mainly introduce the background of this monograph. We first briefly review the history of computer networks to expose the evolution to cloud networking. After that, some representative cloud computing paradigms (e.g., IaaS, PaaS, and SaaS) and the two main types of big data, i.e., batch big data and stream big data, are introduced.

References

1. S. D. Crocker, J. F. Heafner, R. M. Metcalfe, and J. B. Postel, "Function-oriented protocols for the arpa computer network," in *Proceedings of the May 16–18, 1972, spring joint computer conference*. ACM, 1972, pp. 271–279.
2. V. G. Cerf and R. E. Icahn, "A protocol for packet network intercommunication," *ACM SIGCOMM Computer Communication Review*, vol. 35, no. 2, pp. 71–82, 2005.
3. J. Postel, "Ncp/tcp transition plan," 1981.
4. "Internet History," http://compnetworking.about.com/od/history_networking/.
5. "Internet User Counting," http://www.internetlivestats.com/internet-users/.

6. H. Kim and N. Feamster, "Improving network management with software defined networking," *Communications Magazine, IEEE*, vol. 51, no. 2, pp. 114–119, 2013.
7. F. Hu, Q. Hao, and K. Bao, "A survey on software defined networking (sdn) and openflow: From concept to implementation," pp. 1–1, 2014.
8. S. Agarwal, M. Kodialam, and T. Lakshman, "Traffic engineering in software defined networks," in *INFOCOM, 2013 Proceedings IEEE*, IEEE, 2013, pp. 2211–2219.
9. "ONF," https://www.opennetworking.org/.
10. "Data Center Locations," http://www.google.com/about/datacenters/inside/locations/index.html.
11. "IBM Cloud," http://www.ibm.com/cloud-computing/us/en/.
12. "Googlge Computer Engine," https://cloud.google.com/products/compute-engine/.
13. "Amazon EC2," http://aws.amazon.com/ec2/pricing.
14. "DropBox," http://www.dorpbox.com.
15. "ICloud," http://www.icloud.com.
16. "Google Drive," http://www.google-drive.com.
17. "IBM Big Data," http://www.ibmbigdatahub.com/blog/how-internet-things-shaping-modern-business.
18. "IDC Big Data Report," http://www.emc.com/collateral/analyst-reports/idc-the-digital-universe-in-2020.pdf.

Chapter 2
Fundamental Concepts

2.1 Software Defined Networking

2.1.1 Architecture

Today's computer networking is growing ever larger and more complex everyday. This leads to a critical issue on how to manage and control the network devices. SDN is a dynamic, programmable, and scalable framework proposed to provide effective solutions for network behavior management. SDN decouples data plane and control plane, allowing direct programmable controlling and abstraction of the underlying infrastructures. Due to its many advantages, SDN has drawn significant attention from both academical community [1] and industries. For example, Google is building an SDN-based infrastructure to support their Internet services [2]. Many companies like Huawei have already released their SDN products and solutions.

Figure 2.1 gives an overview of SDN architecture. SDN application plane provides APIs for users to directly program and communicate with SDN to customize the network behaviors. An SDN application specifies the network behavior logic, e.g., routing, according to user requirements. The application will be passed down through northbound interface (NBI) between SDN applications and controllers. NBI also provides the abstraction of the networks to SDN controllers to lower the complexity of managing the underlying hardwares. For example, programmers can obtain network status via the provided APIs to enable dynamic provision and management of network resources.

As a logically centralized component, the SDN controllers works as the "brain" of an SDN-based network. SDN control logic may have many different network functions such as network device management, network status monitoring. SDN controller is also editable and accepts new functionalities to support new demands from users. For example, network administrators can implant their self-developed algorithms for globe optimization of SDN networks. As a bridge between the application plane and underling data plane, SDN controller continues to deliver the

© Springer International Publishing Switzerland 2015

D. Zeng et al., *Cloud Networking for Big Data*, Wireless Networks,
DOI 10.1007/978-3-319-24720-5_2

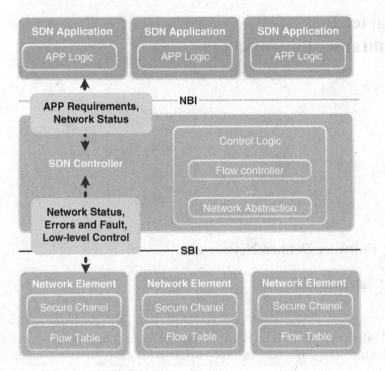

Fig. 2.1 Overview of the SDN architecture

low-level requirements of SDN applications from the control plane down to the data plane to change data forwarding behaviors through the data plane southbound interface (SBI). SBI provides the programmatic control for data forwarding operation, network statistics report, and event notification.

The functionalities of network elements in the data plane can be changed according to the requirements received from the controller through the SBI. The data packet processing behaviors, e.g., forwarding, header alternation, etc., can be altered by updating the flow table in switches and routers. To ensure the secure communication channel between control plane and data plane, OpenFlow protocol is proposed and widely used.

2.1.1.1 OpenFlow

OpenFlow is an open standard proposed and managed by ONF. It specifies a protocol allowing SDN controllers to modify the behavior of networking elements (e.g., OpenFlow switches) through a set of pre-defined instructions or interfaces via a secure channel. A typical OpenFlow switch maintains a flow table for data packet lookup and forwarding.

The flow table contains a set of flow entries including header information to recognize packets and a set of actions that shall be applied to packets. For example, we may define a DDoS prevention scheme by specifying dropping the DDoS attack packets while normal forwarding operation shall be applied to the regular data packets according to the pre-defined actions. The action that shall be applied to a packet can be found out by looking up the flow table. Upon receiving a data packet, OpenFlow switches compare the packet header to the entries in its flow table. If a matching entry is found, OpenFlow switches will perform corresponding actions, in most cases, forwarding the packet to a predetermined port according to the routing scheme. Otherwise, the packet is forwarded to the SDN controller for further decision. In this case, the controller will determine what to do with the packet and add new flow entries to the switches for further actions. The controllers can also update the switch flow tables, e.g., adding new entries and removing existing ones, to meet the SDN application requirements.

2.1.1.2 Ternary Content Addressable Memory

Note that we shall first look up the flow table according to the packet header information to determine what kind of actions shall be applied to the received flow. Consequently, fast lookup is the key to enable fast packet processing. To this end, Ternary Content Addressable Memory (TCAM) is introduced. TCAM is a specified content addressable memory to deal with high-speed searching applications. In OpenFlow switches, it is usually used to store the forwarding tables for fast action lookup. In this case, OpenFlow switches with TCAM can quickly find out the action that shall be applied to the received packet according to its packet header. However, TCAM is notorious for its considerably expensiveness (US$350 for a 1 M-bit chip) and high energy consumption (about 15 Watt/1 Mbit). The TCAM capacity on OpenFlow switch is usually limited and therefore a limited number of forwarding entries can be stored. Most commercial OpenFlow switches, e.g., Broadcom chipset, are with TCAM that can accommodate 750 to 2000 OpenFlow rules. While, modern data centers may have up to 10,000 network flows per second per server rack [3]. Obviously, the limited TCAM size imposes a challenging issue that shall be overcome.

Based on the SDN and OpenFlow technologies, several new projects listed below are proposed to accelerate the network response time and simplify network management.

2.1.2 Floodlight

Floodlight [4] project provides an enterprise-class, Apache-licensed, Java-based OpenFlow controller framework. Many developer and professional engineers have devoted their efforts in the development of Floodlight. It is a user-friendly controller specified to help to manage the increasing switches, routers, virtual switches, and access points. Users without much SDN knowledge can also communicate with the controller and manage the network devices using simple Java programs.

Floodlight has several advantages:

1. It supports mixed network environment with both OpenFlow and non-OpenFlow switches and performs simple and effective management on physical and virtual network devices.
2. It provides user-friendly APIs for SDN controller management using Java language.

Specially, Floodlight has reached a download number of over 6000 times, including large companies like IBM, Arista Networks, Brocade, Dell, Fujitsu, HP, Intel, Juniper Networks, Citrix, and Microsoft [5]. They all actively participate in the development of Floodlight.

2.1.3 OpenDaylight

OpenDaylight [6] is an open source project developed by a group of engineers from different enterprises such as Cisco, IBM, RedHat, and Ericsson. It provides a robust SDN platform allowing further third-party development and innovation. As a main component of SDN, OpenDaylight controller supports flexible management of both physical and virtual networks. Actually, OpenDaylight itself is a powerful SDN platform. Furthermore, the community members are now trying to integrate OpenDaylight with OpenStack Neutron so that both OpenFlow and OpenStack administrators can use this platform. This will provide a powerful SDN-based networking solution for any type of cloud infrastructures.

The main advantages of OpenDaylight are as follows:

1. It supports both OpenFlow and non-OpenFlow switches in physical and virtual forms.
2. It runs within its own Java Virtual Machine (JVM) and therefore can be deployed on any platform that supports Java.
3. It supports REST-style NBIs. That is to say, the OpenDaylight SDN applications can run on different machines from the controller through a web based API.

2.1.4 Ryu SDN Framework

Different from conventional SDN frameworks, Ryu [7] is a component-based framework. Instead of making a full-function heavy controller, Ryu uses a more flexible and lightweighted way, i.e., application component based. Some pre-defined components useful for SDN applications are already implemented and provided in this framework. Users can directly use these existing ones, or combine them to build their own new applications or even implant their self-developed components to realize convenient and more fruitful control of the network devices.

To achieve the component-based application development, Ryu provides user-friendly API for easy creation of new network management and control applications. In addition, Ryu also supports various protocols for managing network devices. Besides OpenFlow, other protocols like Netconf, OF-config, and so on are also supported.

Ryu outperforms other proposals in the following aspects:

1. It has a well-predefined library of components including many frequently used components, e.g., OpenFlow, OpenStack, and firewall.
2. Ryu components are separated and hence it is easier to edit them. Users do not need to read and understand thousands of lines of codes.
3. By reusing different built-in components or even integrating the self-developed new ones, user can easily build new components.

2.2 Network Function Virtualization

In traditional networks, most network functions, such as firewall, deep packet inspection (DPI), gateways, domain name service, are provided by specific hardware in the consideration of fast packet process. With the recent development on the commercial servers, researchers notice that we can still archive fast packet process by the off-the-shelf computers (e.g., X86 servers). This motivates the proposal of Network Function Virtualization (NFV). Via abstracting the purpose-built hardware into software module, traditional network functions can be deployed on a standard computing platform. NFV is applicable to data plane packet processing and control plane function in various types of networks to provide flexible and user customized network functions such as switching elements, tunnelling gateway elements, traffic analysis and scheduling, service assurance.

Figure 2.2 shows an overview of NFV architecture. In essence, a virtualized network function (VNF) is realized by virtualizing the corresponding network function (NFs) (e.g., firewalls, gateways, DNS) as a VM that can apply the same processing logic to the packet going through it. The functions and behaviors of an NF shall not be changed after virtualization. In other words, a physical NF and its corresponding VNF shall have exactly the same functionalities, behaviors, and operational interfaces. Similar to SDN controller, element management systems (EMSs) work as the controlling unit for VNFs.

Both VNF and EMS are built on the NFV infrastructure (NFVI), including both hardware and software. The NFVI can be located in different locations as long as they are connected, e.g., geo-distributed data centers. The physical hardware resources including computing, storage, and network are connected to VNFs in the virtualization layer, which is in charge of abstracting and partitioning hardware resources into virtualized ones.

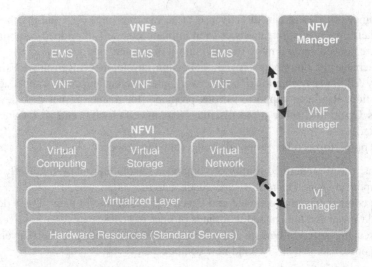

Fig. 2.2 Overview of the NFV architecture

NFV offers many benefits and the most important one is that it can significantly simplify the network as well as the user management. This also further reduces the network CAPEX and OPEX as users do not need to buy expensive purpose-built hardware or no longer need to worry about the multi-version and multi-vendor dedicated hardware with NFV technology. A single general-purpose computing platform is enough for different applications, users, and vendors. This allows network users to share resources across various services and different locations, enabling more network innovations.

NFV technology is mainly applied to two fields, data center and telecommunication. In the next two sections, we briefly introduce how they are adopted and how they benefit the two sectors.

2.2.1   NFV in Data Centers

Today's data centers are facing two challenges: the significantly high OPEX and elastic scalability requirements from users. NFV, as a newly emerging proposal aiming to solve these problems by transforming geo-distributed data centers from IT-centric model to harmonized networking and IT domain model.

NFV makes data centers much more dynamic and even delivers additional benefits such as service innovation acceleration, energy, and cost reduction. Therefore, it is a widely recognized choice for data center infrastructure providers. NFV helps to create efficient data centers to satisfy the demands of service providers and tell them how, where, and when to deploy the services. This creates a reliable, open, and flexible networking environment and makes it easier to manage big data applications. The NFV-based data centers can provide new network functionalities such as policy control and application orchestration for other cloud services. Many network companies like AT&T and Ericsson [8] are now using them for easier and more flexible cloud network management.

Additionally, NFV and data centers also provide an opportunity to better telecommunication services by implementing NFV and moving telecommunication services to the NFV-based IT infrastructures.

2.2.2   NFV in Telecommunications

How to provide fastest and most seamless media experience to users is a key issue to telecommunication service providers. The old solutions cannot satisfy the needs of today's data booming and faster speed demands.

NFV emerges as a promising solution for the telecommunication because it can significantly lower both infrastructure and service costs. By combining with SDN technology, NFV even brings more great economic advantages across all service platforms. For example, Dell [9] is providing NFV solutions for telecommunications providers, cable and mobile operators by leveraging SDN and NFV technologies on their standard X86 servers. This provides an open and vendor-free platform for telecommunication service providers and third-party developers to create their own customized services.

2.3   Relationship Between SDN and NFV

NFV and SDN technologies have much in common. For example, they both provide direct programmability and aim at providing customized controlling and management of the network logically. Moreover, the essential concept of SDN and NFV is the decoupling of the underling infrastructure hardware and software functionality in the network.

Although NFV and SDN technologies share so many features in common, they can be also separately deployed and are even considered as highly complementary to each other as shown in Fig. 2.3. For example, network functions can be virtualized and deployed without an SDN-based network environment. NFV goals can be achieved using non-SDN mechanisms. However, it is without doubt that these two solutions can be combined together. Potentially, greater advantages can be achieved by their marriage. For example, decoupling control and data planes via SDN can improve the performance of NFV by simplifying compatibility in deploying, operation, and maintenance. On the other hand, NFV can provide the standard and uniform infrastructure, where SDN can be installed to manage commodity network elements. Furthermore, NFV can also be applicable to any data plane packet processing and control plane functionalities in SDN-based networks. Potential

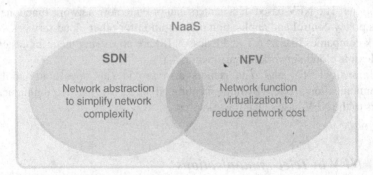

Fig. 2.3 Relationship between SDN and NFV

examples include switches, mobile networks, functions contained in home routers, tunneling gateways, and so on. SDN also provides NFV the opportunity of replacing traditional routing controlling, enabling flexible routing and traffic optimization.

Nevertheless, SDN and NFV together can enable users to optimize their network resources, increase network reliability, accelerate service speed, and create dynamic, user-oriented NaaS.

2.4   Big Data Batch Processing

Like traditional batch processing, big data batch processing solutions also follow the "read-process-write" sequence. Data shall be first read from databases or file systems. They are then processed in computation units. Finally, the obtained results will be written back to databases or file systems. To catch up with the ever-increasing "big data" needs, it is widely agreed that parallelism in big data processing shall be explored to provide faster and scalable services. As a result, many cloud computing oriented parallel computing paradigms have been proposed or even adopted. The most widely used frameworks are listed as follows.

2.4.1   Hadoop

Apache Hadoop [10] is a framework that supports processing of large data sets across clusters of computers using simple programming models. It is designed to leverage the resources of distributed data centers with thousands of machines, offering powerful computation and storage abilities. Many companies and organizations are using Hadoop framework to processing large volume of data every day [11]. The main modules included in this project are Hadoop distributed file system (HDFS) and MapReduce.

2.4.1.1   HDFS

Hadoop is capable of storing large data set by using a distributed file system HDFS which provides high-throughput access to application data. HDFS allows you to store data in distributed storage nodes such as personal computers within one cluster and access them as a seamless system. By storing data to distributed nodes, HDFS frees service providers from purchasing and maintaining their own storage hardware. This not only lowers the data management complexity but also reduces the cost for big data management. HDFS can be applied to heterogeneous hardware and operating systems and has strong reliability since it can detect faults and apply quick, automatic recovery. HDFS also supports parallel processing of the distributed data in different nodes and can place the computation units near the data location to lower the I/O cost. This provides a great opportunity for effective big data processing via careful data placement and task scheduling.

HDFS replicates files for fault tolerance and reliability. Users can customize the number of replicas of a file when it is created and change this number at any time to satisfy their new needs. Usually, three replicas are stored for the same data set. An intelligent replica placement model for reliability and performance is used in HDFS, where a name node controls and optimizes the placement of all replica. A typical HDFS usually consists of large numbers of distributed nodes. The communication costs between them varies according to the physical locations. For example, communication cost between two data nodes in different racks is typically higher than those within the same rack. The name node will try to minimize the communication cost by scheduling the placement of all replica. This significantly simplifies the file management work of users and reduces the communication cost. Figure 2.4 gives a simple example of the modern HDFS with 5 data chunks, each of which has 3 copies stored in different racks.

Compared to other distributed file systems, HDFS has the following noticeable features:

- HDFS uses a "place computation near data" strategy, which greedily places the computation units near the data location. This saves lots of data traffic than traditional moving the data to the computation location.
- HDFS also uses a write-once-read-many model. Once data chunks are written in the storage, they cannot be modified anymore. All the processing will not affect

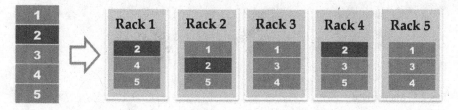

Fig. 2.4 Hadoop file system

the original data. This not only simplifies data coherency but also enables high-throughput data access and fits perfectly for MapReduce applications.

- HDFS always uses one writer at a time for result writing. By such means, the results can be written into the database in orders.
- The replica optimization and rack-aware replica placement policies make HDFS more effective than most other distributed file systems, saving both storage and bandwidth resources.

2.4.1.2 MapReduce

MapReduce is a programming model to distribute the data processing and result generating to the large number of computation nodes (e.g., cloud servers) with a parallel algorithm.

A MapReduce program includes two main phases: *map()* and *reduce()* as shown in Fig. 2.5. The map() filters and sorts data chunks. Take credit card billing data processing as an example. The mappers, the workers who execute map() function, of credit card billing may sort clients' information by their names into queues. After that, these information will be processed in multiple computation units to derive the wanted knowledge for each data split. These inter-mediate results will be stored in the database later. The reducers who execute reduce() function provide a summary operation, e.g., merging the billing information of each client. MapReduce system accelerates big data processing by leveraging the resources in distributed computation units, usually servers. It can run various tasks in parallel, managing communications and data transfers between them, and provide redundancy for fault tolerance.

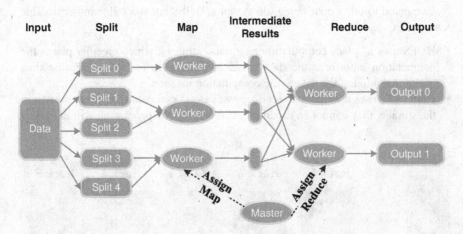

Fig. 2.5 MapReduce

The most important contribution of MapReduce is its scalability and fault-tolerance for different applications. Moreover, MapReduce provides libraries supporting often-used functions written in many programming languages, with different levels of optimization.

However, the MapReduce framework also faces a lot of challenges. Among them, the most critical one is the high communication cost caused by the intermediate result read and merging actions. The MapReduce system can significantly outperform the traditional ones when the network communication cost is minimized.

MapReduce is simple and effective at one-step batch processing. However, it still leads to a lot of I/O processing and is inefficient for multi-step tasks. That is because MapReduce produces a considerable amount of I/O writing and reading in its distributed file system between phases. For example, all intermediate results of present step need to be merged into one and stored in the file system and then these results shall be read from the file system for the next step. To tackle this issue, frameworks supporting multi-step tasks have been proposed, e.g., DIYAD and Spark.

2.4.2 DIYAD

Different from Hadoop, which builds their own new management capabilities, Dryad [12] chooses to leverage the existing cluster management capabilities in Windows HPC servers. Dryad aims to making big data processing easier for application developers using existing resources and knowledge. Unlike Hadoop using a new file system HDFS, Dryad is based on the daily-used and mature New Technology File System (NTFS), which is much easier to use for developers. Additionally, to deal with complex applications, users do not need to carefully join together a sequence of map() and reduce() actions one by one manually. Dryad, on the other hand, allows users to join the complex sequence of MapReduce steps using a simple query language similar to SQL. This greatly reduces the programming load and complexity of developers.

2.4.3 Spark

Apache Spark [13] is an open-source framework developed by the AMPLab at UC Berkeley. Different from Dryad and MapReduce, Spark allows users to load data into a cluster's memory and process it according to users' needs. For example, Spark may perform multiple steps for a single task without writing operations. Spark is well suited to machine learning algorithms and may provide performance up to 100 times faster for some tasks compared to MapReduce.

Spark supports many cluster manager for cluster management, e.g., standalone (native Spark cluster), Hadoop YARN, or Apache Mesos. In the consideration of applicability, Spark also exhibits interfaces targeting for different file systems or databases such as HDFS, Cassandra, OpenStack Swift, and Amazon S3. It is reported that Spark is also the most active big data open source project in Apache software foundation with over 465 contributors in 2014 [14]. Spark core provides distributed task dispatching, scheduling, and basic I/O functionalities. To simplify programming complexity, resilient distributed datasets (RDD) [15], a logical collection of data partitioned across machines, is introduced. Using RDD, users can access the distributed data like local ones. Spark also consists of a streaming component, which leverages Spark core's fast scheduling capability to perform streaming analytics. It divides the stream data as mini-batches and allows RDD transformations on those mini-batches. With Spark streaming, users can apply the old application for batch data to stream ones on the same platform, without changing the source code.

Spark is the first framework to take into consideration stream processing but it is still a general-purpose engine for large-scale data processing and not specifically proposed for stream processing. It allows multiple step processing between data read and result writing actions. However, to read and write data is still very time-consuming and cannot catch up with the speed of stream processing. To deal with the ever-growing demands on real time stream processing, more solutions are proposed specifically for big data stream processing.

2.5 Big Data Stream Processing

Researchers have been attracted by the value of stream processing for big data and some industry companies also try to take advantage of stream data for better strategies and decision making. Unlike big data batch processing, stream processing cannot be simply split and processed in the parallel manner like MapReduce model due to the task sequences and inter-connections. The biggest difference between big data stream processing and the batch ones is that source data are not stored in local file system or database but flow into computation unit in a very fast speed. The stream flow therefore must be processed immediately. Another notable feature of big data stream processing is that it usually requires a sequence of processing steps. In this case, if we continue to use the "process-write" model in batch processing, the I/O communication cost will be extremely high due to the intermediate result writing and read operations. Recent development of in-memory computing motivates us to find solutions for these problems. Via carefully addressing these challenging issues, users including retailers, banks, and large chain stores now can analyze massive data volumes on the fly and perform their actions quickly. The most typical and popular ones are Twitter's Storm and HAMR.

2.5.1 Storm

Twitter Storm [16] is a free and open-source distributed real time computation system for stream data. Potential use cases include real time analytic, online machine learning, and so on. Storm is fast, scalable, fault-tolerant, and easy to set up. Specially, Storm can be used with any programming language. The basic primitives Storm provides for doing stream processing are "spouts" and "bolts" with interfaces for users to implement their own customized logic.

Storm provides spouts for transforming the raw stream data into a new stream in a distributed and reliable way. A new stream in Storm system is a sequence of steps. For example, a spout may receive sensing data from a sensor network and emit them as a new stream. It can also connect directly to the APIs, e.g., Facebook, and emits their raw data as a new stream.

The bolt works as the consumer of streams, performs operations, and then produces result streams for the next bolt without writing them back to file system or database. Bolts can perform various operations such as computation, filter, and data aggregations. As we mentioned, stream processing usually requires multiple steps. For example, for disaster prediction, the sensing data should first be sampled and filtered. The output shall be then sent to a prediction algorithm as input.

An example of spouts and bolts working to process stream data is shown in Fig. 2.6. A processing structure is called as a "topology" in Storm. For different tasks, we shall have different topologies defined by the developers. Each topology can be expressed using a directed acyclic graph (DAG), where a vertex can be a spout or bolt and each edge indicates data flow relationship between the vertices. A spout or bolt producing streams will send the output stream to next step bolt subscribed to them if there is an edge between them. Of course, to deal with the large data volume, both spouts and bolts can execute as many tasks as possible in parallel across data center to explore the bulk cloud computing resources.

Fig. 2.6 Overview of storm

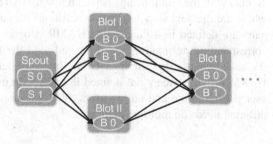

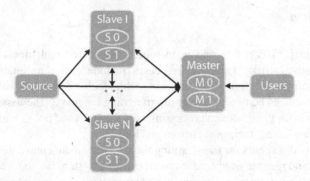

Fig. 2.7 Overview of HAMR

2.5.2 HAMR

HAMR [17] is also a promising solution for big stream data, specially designed for in-memory real time analytics. HAMR's target users are large enterprises, whose business can benefit from its easy to use in-memory and real time processing (Fig. 2.7).

HAMR provides APIs for users to develop their own workflow of stream processing. A client node is provided to handle users' submission of the application workflows. The workflow then is executed through masters and slaves. A master node defines the stream main routine, customized by developer themselves. Once a function is invoked, the workflow will be sent to each slave for processing and transferred back to the master node after completion.

Each slave is only in charge of a part of the workflow, i.e., flowlets. A flowlet can be also divided into a number of partitions to be processed on various processors within one slave, whose behaviors are defined according to corresponding flowlet. To deal with the relationships between flows, HARM uses key/value pairs to define where are the next step destination partitions for each flowlet. When the key/value pairs are defined in a flowlet, the HAMR network layer will find the slaves with corresponding destination partitions and send the key/value pairs to those slaves. By such means, the whole network knows where to send every stream flow. HARM provides many pre-defined flowlets with useful functionalities to simplify user programming and allows users to design more complex processing to satisfy different needs on multiple platforms.

2.6 Summary

In this chapter, we present the main cloud networking enabling technologies, i.e., SDN and NFV, which allow flexible and customizable networking controlling and management. Recent industrial products related to the two technologies (e.g., OpenFlow, Floodlight, OpenDaylight, Ryu Framework, etc.) are also introduced. Representative big data batch processing frameworks (e.g., MapReduce, DIYAD) and stream processing frameworks (e.g., Storm, HAMR) are then introduced, respectively.

References

1. S. Sezer, S. Scott-Hayward, P.-K. Chouhan, B. Fraser, D. Lake, J. Finnegan, N. Viljoen, M. Miller, and N. Rao, "Are we ready for sdn? implementation challenges for software-defined networks," *Communications Magazine, IEEE*, vol. 51, no. 7, pp. 36–43, 2013.
2. "B4: Experience with a Globally-Deployed Software Defined WAN," in *Proc. of ACM SIGCOMM*. ACM, 2013, p. 3–14.
3. T. Benson, A. Akella, and D. A. Maltz, "Network traffic characteristics of data centers in the wild," in *Proceedings of the 10th ACM SIGCOMM Conference on Internet Measurement*. ACM, 2010, pp. 267–280.
4. "FloodLight," http://www.projectfloodlight.org/floodlight/.
5. "FloodLight Developer," http://www.projectfloodlight.org/blog/2012/08/17/floodlight-update/#sthash.UzxQ4vAN.dpuf.
6. "OpenDaylLight," www.opendaylight.org/.
7. "Ryu," http://osrg.github.io/ryu/.
8. "AT&T and Ericsson presenting SDN-based L3VPN solution for Telco NFV needs," http://www.ericsson.com/spotlight/cloud/blog/2015/06/15/att-ericsson-presenting-sdn-based-l3vpn-solution-telco-nfv-needs/
9. "Dell NFV Solution," http://www.dell.com/learn/us/en/04/tme-telecommunications-solutions-telecom-nfv.
10. "Hadoop," http://hadoop.apache.org.
11. "Hadoop Users," http://wiki.apache.org/hadoop/PoweredBy.
12. "Dryad," http://research.microsoft.com/en-us/projects/dryad/.
13. "Spark," http://spark.apache.org/.
14. "Spark User," https://www.openhub.net/p/apache-spark.
15. M. Zaharia, M. Chowdhury, T. Das, A. Dave, J. Ma, M. McCauley, M. J. Franklin, S. Shenker, and I. Stoica, "Resilient distributed datasets: A fault-tolerant abstraction for in-memory cluster computing," in *Proceedings of the 9th USENIX conference on Networked Systems Design and Implementation*. USENIX Association, 2012, pp. 2–2.
16. "Storm," https://storm.apache.org.
17. "HAMR," www.hamrtech.com/.

Chapter 3
Cloud Networking

3.1 Motivation: Fill the Gap Between Application and Network

In the last chapter, we have seen the prosperousness in various big data programming frameworks for either batch data or stream data processing. However, these frameworks still operate on the infrastructure principle in end-to-end fashion evolved from traditional Internet networking where transparent end-to-end transmission services are provided. How data packets are routed in the intermediary devices (e.g., routers) is invisible and uncontrollable. For example, a server in a data center may use either UDP datagrams or TCP sockets as the primary interface to interact with the other servers or to retrieve data from a remote server. On the other hand, the application itself is also almost invisible to the underlying networks. In other words, network and applications reciprocally treat each other as black-boxes. Applications have little controllability via setting few parameters. Actually, this is the design principle of TCP/IP protocol suite. Bearing such concept, an application simply injects a packet and the network just forwards it according to its destination address.

Although such black-box design principle made a huge success in the Internet, the recent rapid development in cloud computing and big data processing expose its shortcomings. It is shown that the inflexibility of black-box design seriously obstructs the efficiency of big data processing in geo-distributed data centers. For example, some recent studies show that data transfer in MapReduce occupies a large portion of the overall job completion time or even becomes the performance bottleneck [1–5]. A recent analysis of MapReduce traces from Facebook reveals that 33 % of the running time of jobs is spent for shuffling data between successive MapReduce stages [1]. It is also reported that 26 % of Facebook's MapReduce jobs are with reduced tasks and the shuffle phase accounts for more than 50 % of the job completion time. In addition, it even accounts for more than 70 % of the running time in 16 % of jobs. This confirms that communication indeed is a non-ignorable issue in MapReduce based big data processing, besides computation and

© Springer International Publishing Switzerland 2015   33
D. Zeng et al., *Cloud Networking for Big Data*, Wireless Networks,
DOI 10.1007/978-3-319-24720-5_3

storage. Poor and unpredictable network performance is particularly detrimental for MapReduce job completion time because MapReduce has some implicit barriers that depend directly on the performance of individual transfers.

Modern data centers intend to promote the inter-server communication efficiency by providing high-capacity bisection links and alternative multiple paths. Nevertheless, traditional general network oriented protocols fail to explore such advantages. For example, TCP/IP usually assumes a single path between the communication end hosts and uses other alternative paths only in case of failure. This is a direct outcome of end-to-end black-box design principle. In spite of its success in traditional networks with only a few paths between hosts, the potential of modern data center networks is under-utilized. To address this issue, some new forwarding protocols like ECMP (Equal Cost Multi-path) [6] are proposed. Although with improved efficiency, these new forwarding protocols essentially are still limited due to the obliviousness of individual application's traffic characteristics, leading to performance degradation. Therefore, it is highly desiderated that the network can be programmed at runtime such that communications can be optimized for faster, service-aware, and more resilient application execution, specially for the communication-intensive applications such as big data processing. This creates a strong motivation for a new networking paradigm that fills the gap between applications and underlying networks. Fortunately, with the recent progress in networking technologies as reviewed in the last chapter, solid foundation has been built for creating new networking paradigm to overcome these limitations.

3.2   Cloud Networking Architecture

With the consideration of big data processing requirements and the enabling technologies such as SDN and NFV, we envision a three-layer cloud networking architecture shown in Fig. 3.1. The *application layer* provides a programming interface between end users and underlying physical resources. The middle *control layer* performs as a middlebox for resource abstraction and management. *Infrastructure* refers to physical resources, including physical computation, communication, storage, and energy resources. The main functions of the components in control layers are detailed as follows.

3.2.1   Parser and Scheduler

Parser is in charge of analyzing the application requirements on various kinds of resources. Different resource provision policies can be specified by programmers through the networking programming interfaces (NPIs) provided by the parser. For example, we may incorporate SDN's NBIs as a subset of NPIs to enable SDN-based network control and management. We may also use the OpenStack's APIs to acquire

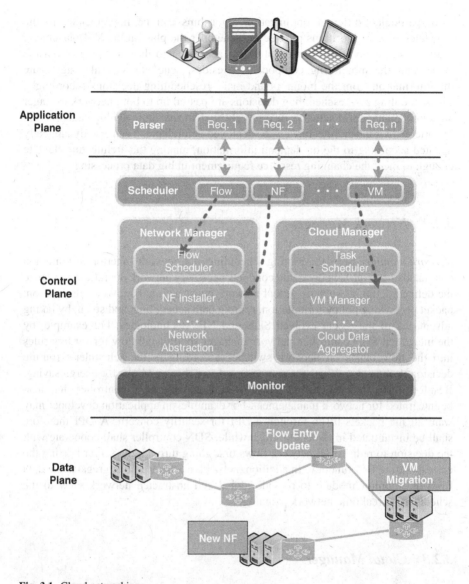

Fig. 3.1 Cloud networking

desired network of VMs for building cloud applications. The parser then interprets these high-level specifications into the commands that can be executed by *scheduler* module component, which is responsible for resource allocation. It receives the requirements from the parser and reacts according to the real time information from the monitoring components to make the decisions such as where a VM shall be placed or migrated, which path a flow shall be routed, and what kind of network function shall be instantiated.

In particular, different optimization algorithms can be implemented in the scheduler. These algorithms provide the scheduler the plan on the VM placement, routing and network function instantiation according to the knowledge from the parser and the monitoring components. Besides, scheduler can also aggregate the information from the monitors and make rescheduling decisions accordingly. The scheduling and rescheduling decisions are passed up to both network manager and cloud manager for actual realization. By such means, not only big data processing oriented virtual architecture can be deployed beforehand, it can also dynamically updated according to the on-demand information, making the architecture flexible enough to meet the changing resource requirement in big data processing.

3.2.2   Network Manager

Network manager takes the routing scheduling and network function instantiation commands from the scheduler and conducts necessary network operations to realize the defined activities such as virtual network construction, bandwidth reservation, packet processing policy formulation, routing path scheduling, and so on, by taking advantages of the recent evolved SDN and NFV technologies. For example, by the integrated SDN controller, network manager shall install flow forwarding rules into the flow tables on network switches according to the scheduler's routing decision. It may also deactivate some unused switches and links for energy saving. Besides SDN controller for network flow management, NFV controller shall also be integrated for network management. For example, an application developer may want all the packets to go through a DPI for security concern. A DPI therefore shall be instantiated in the cloud. Meanwhile, SDN controller shall cooperate with the decision to redirect all network flows first going through the server hosting the corresponding DPI function. In addition, network manager also aggregates the data from the monitor module to provide global and abstracted network view to the scheduler for real time network planning.

3.2.3   Cloud Manager

As an important part of the network manager, *cloud manager* is in charge of task and server resource (i.e., computation and storage) management. It acts as a bridge to realize operations, such as task construction, task deconstruction, VM placement, VM migration, data placement, data migration, and so on, in response to the commands from the scheduler. It enables dynamic cloud resource provision and further makes cloud resources response to ever-changing demands easily and quickly as developers can reschedule virtual servers using given interfaces. Many issues jointly affect the system performance and efficiency. For example, to enable high quality-of-experience for a cloud service, we may deploy as many VMs as we can and assign corresponding tasks on these VMs. Task scheduler and VM manager shall be responsible for such issues. In addition, we may also dynamically change the virtualized service infrastructure to react to the changing workloads. Therefore, similar to the network manager, the cloud manager also checks status of all the servers, virtual machines, and tasks, then reports relevant information back to the scheduler during runtime for rescheduling.

3.2.4 Monitor

Monitor component monitors the running status of tasks, flow statistics at routers, server and router statuses in the cloud computing platform. It is of great importance to dynamic resource provision. It may periodically polling both the routers and servers to obtain the required information or asks the routers and servers to actively report their statuses. For example, both the servers and routers track the ingress and egress network traffic over their network interfaces. These data are reported to the network manager. We may also implement Hadoop runtime monitor for collecting the application-level information at each server. Besides actual monitoring, monitoring component is also able to predict the future resource requirements according to the past and present information of the request pattern, task processing statuses, server statuses, etc. All the monitoring information, either from actual sampling or machine-learning based prediction, is essential for the scheduler to make appropriate management decisions to the underlying infrastructure according to the application needs.

3.3 Design Issues

3.3.1 Language Abstractions

To fill the gap between the application and the network, the first requirement is on the programming issue. Uniform and high level description of the infrastructure resources and user requirements is needed, making programmers not worry about the low-level details in the infrastructure hardware, including both servers and routers. Developers can easily write programs using the specified language to acquire needed resources and capture intended operation behavior of underlying hardware. A compiler that is able to transform these specifications into code segments for both servers and network devices is needed. To support orchestration on the infrastructure according to the big data processing requirements, fruitful language abstractions shall be provided, such as:

1. System query abstractions: As we have known, the monitor module can provide various monitoring information about runtime statuses of both the servers and

the network devices. To enable the developers to easily get these information for user-defined scheduling and rescheduling, system query abstractions must be provided. For example, an OpenFlow switch may store the counters associated with different forwarding rules or flows, making the programmers able to understand the networking behavior in fine grain.

2. Virtual network topology construction: It is desirable that the underlying architecture can be customized according to the big data processing needs. One of the main principles of cloud computing is sharing. Besides virtualization technology enabled server sharing, via cloud networking, the network hardware resources shall be shared among the users, who are with different demands. Network virtualization is a key technology to pursue such requirement. Abstraction to enable virtual network topology construction shall be constructed.

3. Network function instantiation. With cloud computing, besides constructing the virtual network topology according to the big data processing requirements, we shall also allow the programmers to instantiate different network functions, e.g., network address translation, firewall, DNS, DPI, etc., in the network. High-level network function abstraction therefore shall be provided.

4. VM operation abstraction. Cloud networking does not only focus on the networking itself, it is highly recommended that the computation, storage, and communication can be considered in a joint manner. Therefore, abstraction to the VM operation shall also be provided. Via such abstraction, programmers can jointly orchestrate all hardware resources in one control program, enabling more innovations.

3.3.2 Performance Optimization

System performance is always of the first concern in any system. In big data processing, especially the big data stream processing, speed is critical to the quality of data processing. Cloud networking enables flexible control of various network resources. Further with the server abstraction, it is possible that we can optimize the overall system performance by jointly consideration of task allocation, VM placement, data placement, routing scheduling, and network function deployment. Together with the hardware abstractions, all resources can be rescheduled according to the application requirement. System-level resource management mechanism and processing system control shall be established for big data. This radically changes the vision of resource allocation and scheduling towards performance promotion. For example, there is no pure end-to-end traffic engineering any more. All computation, storage, and communication resources shall be jointly considered towards performance optimization.

Besides static optimization, we may also require runtime optimization according to the statistics from the monitor module. Therefore, we shall be able to quickly and dynamically modify previous configurations of the infrastructure to accommodate new demands. Direct hardware reconfiguration is slow, difficult, and expensive, failing to catch up with the "velocity" of big data. The "software definable" cloud networking provides a promising solution and we shall elaborately leverage such technology to dynamically optimize the system performance to catch up with the increasing needs of big data.

3.3.3   Energy and Cost Optimization

Besides the performance issue, the system efficiency is also non-ignorable. System efficiency directly affects the energy consumption and expenditure. Gartner predicts that the total CAPEX on hardware investment worldwide on data centers will surpass 177 billion dollars by 2015. Besides the CAPEX, the OPEX is also considerably high, specially due to the extremely high energy consumption of large-scale data centers. As shown in [7], electricity cost has become the dominant OPEX, even surpassing the CAPEX to service providers and is rising every year. With the increasing data volume and analytical demands, the processing, storage, and transmission of big data will inevitably consume more and more electric energy. As show in this figure form a white book of Intel, the cost of data centers increases every year. Gartner predicts that by 2015, 71 % of worldwide data center hardware spending will come from the big data processing, which will surpass $126.2 billion. Big data nowadays is equivalent to big cost (Fig. 3.2). Lowering data center cost has therefore become a major concern. Obviously, similar to the performance issue, the energy and cost efficiency requires a heavy consolidation of both computing and network resources meanwhile deeply related to the performance issue as we must guarantee the predetermined quality of service (QoS).

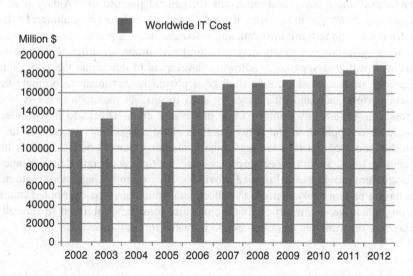

Fig. 3.2 Data center cost

3.3.4   Flexible Data Management

The significant increasing data deluge in the big data era requires new solutions on data access, storage, and management. To support storage and management of large data chunks, distributed file systems like HDFS have been proposed and widely used. However, existing file systems are strictly designed with a lack of scalability and flexibility, hence could not satisfy the required performance to obey SLA. More flexible user-definable data storage system is advocated. For example, in HDFS, certain redundancy of data chunks is required to ensure the data security. However, how to utilize these redundancy is not regulated. Via cloud networking, we shall freely balance the workload by orienting the access paths to leverage these redundancy. By such means, not only the data security is guaranteed, the system may also become more efficient. Of course, to achieve this goal, many issues like redundancy level, load balancing solution, data access route, and data placement need to be addressed as they directly affect both system performance and efficiency.

3.3.5   Stream Processing Aware Network Resource Management

Different from the relatively slow change of pre-storage data systems, real time stream data, e.g., sensor streams, stock market data streams, chain store sales streams, etc., are continuously generated at unprecedented rates. Present batch data oriented data processing framework is not suitable any more. Although some specific stream processing frameworks are proposed and implemented. These frameworks hide many low-level details for general purpose use. Although such manner makes programming easier, it is not flexible enough for programmers to efficiently use the underlying infrastructure resources in an application-oriented way. In stream processing, a stream may go through a number of different processing units with different semantics. Allowing developers to determine the number of processing units and where they shall be deployed is significant to promote the system performance and efficiency. By such means, an inevitable issue is how to route the stream flows among these processing units. Thanks to the seamless integration of application and networking via cloud networking, we can carefully plan this and program it according to the application characteristics. Besides the processing units, stream processing may have multiple cooperative data sources, infrastructure providers, and service providers. For example, chain store customer purchasing pattern analysis needs to collect data from many geo-distributed stores. A comprehensive stream processing architecture must be established to carefully orchestrate the available data sources and infrastructure resources.

3.3.6 Security

Data security is essential in big data processing. Cloud networking allows users to customize any network topology integrated with different network functions in one shared physical network. It delivers optimization opportunities but also a challenge how to ensure the data security of big data processing. For example, the credit card billing data contain some sensitive personal information and the details of customers' purchasing. The challenge comes from the fact that the developers shall be responsible for data security guaranteeing since the networks are programmable. On the other hand, fortunately, cloud networking is a promising technology for adding network level intelligence in the consideration of data security. For example, we can freely deploy DPI functions or firewalls via NFV technology as needed. We may also apply SDN to customize the routing paths, monitor data traffic, diagnose threats, and migrate security challenges.

3.4 Cloud Networking and Big Data Related Work Review

With the recent networking technology evolution and emerging big data processing requirements, many efforts have been devoted to develop these emerging technologies and leverage these technologies to achieve various optimization goals. These studies provide us precious results and experiences on how to improve the cloud networking and how to leverage cloud networking for big data processing optimizations. We summarize some recent representative work in different areas as follows.

3.4.1 Energy and Cost Reduction

A large number of data centers are being operated by cloud service providers such as Google, Microsoft, and Amazon. According to [8], a data center may consist of thousands of servers and consume megawatts of power. Millions of dollars on electricity cost have posed a heavy burden on the OPEX to data center providers. Therefore, reducing the electricity cost has received significant attention from both academia and industry, and many technologies and schemes have been proposed to decrease the energy consumption and electricity cost in data centers [8–11]. Among the mechanisms that have been proposed so far for data center energy management, the techniques that attract lots of attention is data center resizing (DCR). DCR is a mechanism to reduce energy consumption by changing the numbers of activated servers in each data center. By DCR, the unused servers are put into sleeping state or even shutdown to save energy and hence the electricity cost. Although DCR mainly refers to the activation/deactivation of servers, it is also highly correlated with communications as DCR is usually jointly investigated with task (or request) dispatching. The tasks can be only distributed to the activated servers. In 2010, Rao et al. [12] publish their work on how to reduce electricity cost by routing user requests to geo-distributed data centers with accordingly updated sizes that match the requests. Later, Liu et al. [13] re-examine the same problem by taking network delay into consideration.

With the possibility of dynamic workload distribution and scheduling, we can also explore the electricity price heterogeneity for OPEX reduction. Geo-distributed data centers have various electricity prices and processing abilities. Distributing more workloads to data centers with lower price and higher processing abilities can potentially reduce the total electricity cost, provided that the predefined QoS is guaranteed. Request mapping dynamically dispatches workloads across all available data centers to exploit electricity price heterogeneities. Gao et al. [14] propose optimal workload control and balancing by taking account of access latency, carbon footprint, and electricity costs. In the same year, Liu et al. [15] published their work on reducing electricity cost and environmental impact using a holistic approach of workload balancing that integrates renewable supply, dynamic pricing, and cooling supply. Later, Delimitrou et al. [16] present Paragon, a heterogeneity- and interference-aware online DC scheduler, which is derived from robust analytical methods, instead of by profiling each application.

To reduce the energy consumption and lower the OPEX, dynamic workload distribution is inevitably needed. Cloud networking technique is quite helpful to enable service developers to program the network according to the optimization objectives. As we have known, load balancing can be easily realized via controlling the routing behaviors to balance the workloads.

3.4.2   VM Placement

With virtualization technology, physical machines (PMs) in data centers, i.e., servers, are organized as VMs with specific types, to meet requirements of various cloud service providers. User requests can be only distributed to these types of VMs that are deployed by the corresponding service provider. In modern data centers, servers are virtualized into several types of VMs with corresponding physical resources to process different user requests. VMs in data centers have been widely investigated in the literature. For example, Liu et al. [17] propose GreenCloud architecture which enables comprehensive online-monitoring, live VM migration, and VM placement optimization towards energy minimization. Besides the consideration on the energy efficiency issue, Meng et al. [18] improve the network scalability by optimizing the traffic-aware VM placement according to the traffic patterns among VMs. Cohen et al. [19] also study the problem of VM placement for the traffic intense data centers, but with a goal of maximizing the benefit (i.e., demand satisfaction) from the overall communication sent by the VMs to a single designated point in the data center.

Task distribution and VM placement are two mostly used methods to improve the data center performance and utility. Xu et al. [20] propose a two-level control system to manage the mappings of workloads to VMs and VMs to physical resources. They treat the VM placement problem as a multi-objective optimization problem in order to simultaneously minimize total resource wastage, power consumption, and thermal dissipation cost. Jiang et al. [21] study joint tenant (e.g., server or virtual machine) placement and routing problem to minimize traffic costs and propose an efficient online algorithm in a dynamic environment under changing traffic loads. Later, Zeng et al. [22] address the problem of VM placement to minimize the aggregated communication cost within a data center under the consideration of both architectural and resource constraints.

It can be seen that workload distribution shall also be considered in VM placement and migration. Via cloud networking, we can control the workload distribution in a fine-grained manner. Today's data centers host online services on multiple servers, with a front-end load balancer directing each client request to a particular replica. Dedicated load balancers are expensive and quickly become a single point of failure and congestion. Wang et al. [23] propose a proactive server load balancing approach by leveraging SDN to proactively install *wildcard* rules in the switches to direct requests for large groups of clients, without involving the controller. A binary tree representation of IP prefix is used to implement their design. Besides, from these related studies, we can see that VM placement or migration has deep influence on many communication issues, e.g., service response latency, communication cost, traffic congestion, etc. Therefore, we shall investigate VM placement/migration with the consideration of networking. We can specify the network policy via cloud networking, together with VM placement/migration, to achieve various performance and efficiency goals.

3.4.3　Big Data Placement

Big data services are characterized by its large storage and communication resource requirements. The first key issue in big data management is reliable and effective data placement. To achieve this goal, Sathiamoorthy et al. [24] present a novel family of erasure codes that are efficiently repairable and offer higher reliability compared to Reed-Solomon codes. They also analytically show that their codes are optimal on an identified tradeoff between locality and minimum distance. Yazd et al. [25] make use of flexibility in the data block placement policy to increase energy efficiency in data centers and propose a scheduling algorithm, which takes into account energy efficiency in addition to fairness and data locality properties. Hu et al. [26] propose a mechanism allowing linked open data to take advantage of existing large-scale data stores to meet the requirements on distributed and parallel data processing. Moreover, how to allocate the computation resources to tasks has also drawn much attention. Cohen et al. [27] present new design philosophy, techniques, and experience providing a new magnetic, agile, and deep data analysis for one of the world's largest advertising networks at Fox Audience Network, using the Greenplum parallel database system. Kaushik et al. [28] propose a novel, data-centric algorithm to reduce energy costs and with the guarantee of thermal-reliability of the servers. Chen et al. [29] consider the problem of jointly scheduling all three phases, i.e., map, shuffle, and reduce, of the MapReduce process and propose a practical heuristic to combat the high scheduling complexity. Agarwal et al. [30] propose an automated data placement mechanism Volley for geo-distributed cloud services with the consideration of WAN bandwidth cost, data center capacity limits, data inter-dependencies, etc. Cloud services make use of Volley by submitting logs of datacenter requests. Volley analyzes the logs using an iterative optimization algorithm based on data access patterns and client locations, and outputs migration recommendations back to the cloud service. Shachnai et al. [31] investigate how to determine a placement of Video-on-Demand (VoD) file copies on the servers and the amount of load capacity assigned to each file copy so as to minimize the communication cost while ensuring the user experience. Cidon et al. [32] invent MinCopysets, a data replication placement scheme that decouples data distribution and replication to improve the data durability properties in distributed data centers. Recently, Jin et al. [33] propose a joint optimization scheme that simultaneously optimizes VM placement and network flow routing to maximize energy savings.

Data placement also has deep impact on the network performance and efficiency, especially those data-intensive big data applications. Similar to VM placement/migration, it is not an independent issue either. A service provider shall jointly consider both data placement and network management. Again, cloud networking provides such possibility to program the network simultaneously with data placement specification.

3.4.4   Big Data Stream Processing

Besides big batch data processing, big data stream processing is a new challenge which is attracting researchers' attention in the literature from different aspects. The study on stream data processing started from many years ago. In 2002, Humphreys et al. [34] gave examples of real-world applications that use Chromium to achieve good scalability on clusters of workstations, and describe other potential uses of this stream processing technology. Cherniack et al. [35] propose a centralized stream processor "Aurora," in which for each ad hoc query there is a deterministic flow graph. Tian et al. [36] study a resource allocation problem in stream environment with the goal of network utility maximization but the dependency between nodes in the stream workflow is not considered. He et al. [37] reveal strong temporal and spatial correlations among queries and propose Comet that is able to significantly eliminate I/O redundancies and temporal load imbalance. Zhao et al. [38] propose a unified modeling framework for distributed fork and join processing, based on which they formulate resource allocation problem into an optimization problem and solve it using a distributed back-pressure based algorithm.

Task placement (also referred to as operator placement) has attracted significant interests in the distributed stream processing systems community. Lakshmanan et al. [39] propose a placement strategy for stateless tasks in order to improve the performance of the message processing.

Different from conventional stream processing studies, big data stream processing is characterized by its big data volume and fast data rate. Therefore, public clouds, or geo-distributed data centers, are explored to provide computation and communication resources. One of the leading elements of IBM portfolio in stream processing is InfoSphere Streams [40], a versatile, high-performance, and cost effective solution that manages and analyzes massive volume, variety, and velocity of data that consumers and businesses create every day. [41] is an Apache-based Storm processing handler with fully certified component of Hortonworks data platform. It provides customers with stream processing for real time analysis of some of the most common new types of data such as sensor and machine data. Amazon also provides Kinesis [42], by which users can call for large-scale, real time data ingestion and processing in any situation. Logs for servers and other IT infrastructure, social media or market data feeds, web clickstream data, and the like are all great candidates for processing with Kinesis. Another famous framework called Spark [13] is an open source, parallel data processing framework that complements Apache Hadoop to make it easy to develop fast, unified big data applications combining batch, stream, and interactive analytics. Data Torrent [43] is a next-generation in-memory stream framework that can process huge amounts of data in a reliable, enterprise-worthy manner.

Without doubt that stream processing has a strong relationship with the networking issue as large volume of data may be transferred between different processors. How the communication performs directly affects the overall performance and efficiency. However, existing frameworks, like Storm and Spark, they still treat the network as a blackbox, leaving no space for developers to optimize the communications. Cloud computing fills such gap by providing NPIs such that the network can be programmed according to the stream processing needs, together with the actual application development.

3.4.5   Big Data Aware Traffic Cost Optimization

Cloud networking can be applied in geo-distributed data centers. There are many recent studies on traffic cost minimization in geo-distributed data centers focusing on routing strategies and resource optimization. Regarding cloud providers' operational costs on network traffic, Zhang et al. [44] design a routing algorithm using the flow-based model to optimize the costs on DC-to-client traffic in each time interval. Laoutaris et al. [45] propose NetStitcher, which explores the under-utilized bandwidth at night to transfer bulk data among data centers through store-and-forward approach to reduce inter-DC traffic cost. Feng et al. [46] propose Postcard to minimize the network cost of multiple source-destination traffic pairs. Postcard is also in the concept of store-and-forward via leveraging the intermediate data centers. Fang et al. [47] present a novel approach, called VMPlanner, for network power reduction in the virtualization-based data centers. The basic idea of VMPlanner is to jointly optimize virtual machine placement and traffic flow routing so as to turn off as many unneeded network elements as possible for power saving. Lee et al. [48] propose an architecture that adopts a "what if" methodology to guide allocation decisions taken by the IaaS. The architecture uses a prediction engine with a lightweight simulator to estimate the performance of a given resource allocation and a genetic algorithm to find an optimized solution in the large search space. Corradi et al. [49] focus on it from a more practical viewpoint, with specific attention on the consolidation aspects related to power, CPU, and networking resource sharing using OpenStack. Moreover, they propose a cloud management platform to optimize VM consolidation along three main dimensions, namely power consumption, host resources, and networking. A virtual execution environment, consisting of VMs interconnected with virtual networks, provides opportunities to dynamically optimize, at run-time, the performance of existing, unmodified distributed applications without any user or programmer intervention is proposed by Sundararaj et al. [50]. Lange et al. [51] propose VTL which is a framework for packet modification and creation whose purpose is to modify network traffic to and from a VM, doing so transparently to the VM and its applications. Calcavecchia et al. [52] provide a practical model of cloud placement management under a stream of requests and present a novel technique called Backward Speculative Placement (BSP) that projects the past demand behavior of a VM to a candidate target host. [53] focus on satisfying the traffic demands of the VMs in addition to CPU and memory requirements. This is a much more complex problem both due to its quadratic nature (being the communication between a pair of VMs) and since it involves many factors beyond the physical host, like the network topologies and the routing scheme.

It can be seen that most traffic optimization studies mentioned above more or less are related to VMs. This falls into the design concept of cloud networking that the networking shall not be treated as a blackbox, but shall be jointly considered with the computation hosts, e.g., VMs. According to our cloud networking architecture, it is possible to put all these resources in one pool such that programmers or developers can easily manages using the given APIs. This potentially promotes the flexibility and hence the efficiency.

3.4.6 SDN Aware Optimization

As a key enabling technology to cloud networking, SDN plays an important role and has also been attracting much attention in the research communication. Many studies have been proposed from different aspects. We briefly summarize some of them as follows.

3.4.6.1 SDN-Based Routing Optimization

Some recent initiatives leverage SDN to optimize data flow routing and perform load balancing among the available multiple paths. For example, Agarwal et al. [54] show how to leverage the centralized controller to get significant improvements in network utilization as well as to reduce packet losses and delays. The core concept is to manipulate the network traffic that passes through the SDN forwarding element in hybrid SDN networks where the SDN switches and conventional switches coexist, as SDN switches are incrementally deployed. Jain et al. [55] explain key reasons for virtualization and briefly explain several of the networking technologies that have been developed recently or are being developed in various standard bodies. In particular, they illustrate SDN's applicability with their own research on OpenADN application delivery in a multi-cloud environment. Hong et al. [56] present SWAN that boosts the utilization of inter-data center networks by centrally controlling the network traffic load according to the traffic demand. They leverage a small amount of scratch capacity on links to apply multi-stage updates in a provably congestion-free and order-oblivious manner. They also classify the cloud services into three types: interactive, elastic, and background, with different traffic characteristics. Besides applying SDN to the backbone networks or data center networks, recently, Lee et al. [57] propose meSDN that extends SDN capability to mobile end devices so as to provide true end-to-end software-defined solutions for network problems.

To big data processing, systems such as Hedera [58], MicroTE [59], Mahout [60] and DARD [61] are proposed. They all implement a flow scheduler and use current network load statistics to estimate traffic demands and dynamically redistribute flows among the available paths.

Hedera [58] dynamically schedule flows among the multipaths in data center networks with the goal of maximizing aggregated network utilization. Hedera is motivated by the observation that the large elephant flows may cause network bottlenecks and severely degrade the system performance if they are not well scheduled. Hedera leverages a global view of the routing and traffic demands. A flow-level information is proposed to enable the scheduler to detect elephant flow whose rate is beyond a predefined threshold. By estimating how much bandwidth the elephant needs, the controller computes the available nonconflicting paths and instructs the associated switches to re-route the detected elephant flows according to ease the burden on the congested paths.

Mahout [60] relies on the same ideas behind Hedera to maximize the aggregate network utilization. However, it overcomes Hedera's performance limitations by pushing the large flow detection to the end-hosts and using an inband signaling mechanism. A key idea of the Mahout system is to monitor end-host's socket buffers for elephant flow detection. It relies on the fact that applications fill the TCP buffers at a rate much higher than the observed network rate. Once one or more elephant flows are detected, a central controller uses placement algorithms to compute good paths for them and instructs switches to reroute traffic accordingly. This is similar to Hedera, but with the difference that in Mahout the elephant flow detection happens sooner and in the end-host.

Beson et al. [59] propose MicroTE relying on fact that many flows in a data center are with predictable traffic demands. MicroTE is a fine-grained multipath flow scheduling approach that leverages short-term traffic prediction and a global view of the network to reschedule flows so as to mitigate the congestion caused by the unpredictable traffic.

DARD (Distributed Adaptive Routing for Data centers) [61] is a flow scheduling system that allows each end-host to move traffic from overloaded to underloaded paths. Unlike the other systems described earlier, DARD does not require central coordination. Instead, it lets end-hosts select paths based only on their local knowledge and uses a game theory inspired algorithm to achieve global optimization goals. Once an elephant flow is detected, DARD has to decide if this flow should be moved to a different path or not.

3.4.6.2   SDN Aware Energy Optimization

Via SDN, we can flexibly orchestrate the available networking resources to promote the system performance. Besides, it is also possible to leverage it for energy optimization and many efforts have been already devoted to this area.

Wang et al. [62] propose CARPO, a correlation-aware power optimization algorithm that dynamically consolidates traffic flows onto a small set of links and switches in a data center networks and then shuts down unused network devices for energy savings. CARPO is designed based on a key observation by analyzing real data center network traces that the bandwidth demands of different flows do not peak at exactly the same time. As a result, if the correlations among flows are considered in consolidation, more energy savings can be achieved. In addition, CARPO integrates traffic consolidation with link rate adaptation to further maximize energy savings.

Wang et al. [63] propose a novel energy saving model for data center networks by scheduling and routing "deadline-constrained flows" where the transmission of every flow has to be accomplished before a rigorous deadline. They characterize the energy optimization problem with a time-aware model and solve it by assigning VMs to servers to reduce the amount of traffic and to generate favorable conditions for traffic engineering for reducing the number of active switches and balancing traffic flows.

Li et al. [64] propose an SDN-based energy-aware routing called exclusive routing (EXR) for data center networks. Instead of letting the flows fairly share the bandwidth, EXR sets different priorities of flows and makes them exclusively occupy the communication links in order to promote the link utilizations and hence the energy efficiency.

3.4.6.3   Programming and Abstraction

PaaS eases cloud deployment by automating placement decisions, scaling, and maintenance of the infrastructure. Yet, most PaaS offers limited network support to HTTP and application development needs other protocols that can hardly be used. To address this problem, Kachele et al. [65] propose COSCAnet as a PaaS-cloud network layer that virtualizes socket interfaces for UDP and TCP. In [66], Jain et al. present the design, implementation, and evaluation of B4, a private WAN connecting Google's data centers across the planet. It can be seen that a new form of network programming is demanded the big data era. Nunes et al. [67] survey the state-of-the-art in programmable networks, with an emphasis on SDN. Many OpenFlow standard compliant software switch (e.g., Open vSwitch [68], Pantou/OpenWRT [69] etc.) and controller (e.g., POX [70], OVS-Controller [68], etc.) implementations are summarized and compared.

   To SDN programming, how to specify the rules in the programmable switches plays a key role. Consequently, some studies are also devoted to programming abstraction and optimization on rule specification. In SDN, the controller responds for installing flow-based rules at switches in either reactive or proactive approach. The reactive approach allows controller applications to dynamically manage network flows at runtime according to realtime traffic demands and network conditions. However, it performs worse than the proactive one due to the involvement of controller. In the proactive approach, the controller installs rules in switches beforehand for all the flows going through these switches. However, the proactive approach requires a priori knowledge of traffic shapes and network conditions at all switches. Obviously, reactive approach is more flexible and elastic than the proactive one. To reduce the controller involvement in reactive approach for performance promotion, many studies recognize the limitations of flow-based rules and have proposed data plane oriented optimizations. DevoFlow [71] reduces the controller overhead by introducing rule cloning and measurement triggers. OpenFlow 1.3 supports rate limiting by allowing switches to track flow rates and tag/drop excess traffic without the controller involvement. Open vSwitch [68] allows software switches to install new rules when traffic matches an old rule. Moshref et al. [72] propose FAST (Flow-level State Transitions) as a switch abstraction that allows the controller to proactively program state transitions, and allows switches to run dynamic actions based on local information.

3.4.6.4   SDN Rule Management

Forwarding table in an SDN-enabled switch often relies on TCAM memory, which is expensive and limited. To address this problem and efficiently use these limited TCAM memory, many methods have been proposed in the literature.

   It is highly recommended that multipath routing shall be used in data center networks to explore the potential of multiple coexisting paths between communication ends. However, when SDN is incorporated, although it takes in many benefits, some new constraints are also added in. Giroire et al. [73] notice that if we use 15-shortest paths between each pair of switches (as in MPLS) for fully network capacity exploration, installing these tunnels needs up to 20K rules at switches while off-the-shelf Broadcom Trident2 chipset supports only 16K OpenFlow rules. They present an ILP formulation on the SDN-based energy-aware routing via minimizing the number of activated links and specially address the issue that the OpenFlow switch can hold a finite number of rules. Nguyen et al. [74] argue that it is essential to respect the endpoint policy (i.e., reach the desired set of egress points for an ingress point). They therefore study rule placement strategy to maximize the value of the traffic that respects the endpoint policy in SDNs via trading routing for better efficiency. The switch memory capacity constraints are considered. Cohen et al. [75] investigate the effect of forwarding table size on the network utilization. They formulate the problem into a bounded path-degree max-flow problem which is described using LP. They describe the rule capacity constraints on each switch as path-degree constraints and assume pre-known paths between communication pairs. The available paths that can be selected for traffic routing are limited by forwarding table sizes.

Yu et al. [76] propose DIFANE, a scalable and efficient solution that keeps all traffic in the data plane by selectively directing packets through intermediate switches that store the necessary rules. DIFANE relegates the controller to simply partition these rules among the managed switches. DIFANE uses auxiliary TCAMs as secondary caches to the switches already in the network.

Kanizo et al. [77] introduce Palette distribution framework for decomposing large SDN tables into small ones and distributing these subtables onto appropriate switches so as to balance the sizes of tables across the network and reduce the total number of entries. Two table decomposing algorithms, Pivot Bit Decomposition (PBD) and Cut-Based Decomposition (CBD), are proposed. The subtable distributing problem is modelled into a *rainbow path problem* to decide the colors (equivalent to subtables) that shall be allocated to a node (equivalent to switch). Each path traverses all tables at least once (requirement). Later, Kang et al. [78] propose a method that can minimize the number of rules needed to realize the end point policy. They propose a rectangular representation of the endpoint policy and a rule allocation scheme based on LP. They also advocate that three-tier abstraction for SDN as (1) high-level SDN applications should define their end-point connectivity policy on top of switch abstraction; (2) a mid-level SDN infrastructure layer should decide on the hop-by-hop routing policy; and (3) a compiler should synthesize an effective set of forwarding rules that obey the user-defined policies and adhere to the resource constraints of the underlying hardware.

Katta et al. [79] think that any infinite SDN switch must satisfy four core criteria: (1) elasticity (combining the best of hardware and software switches), (2) transparency (supporting native OpenFlow semantics faithfully), (3) fine-grained rule caching (placing popular rules in the TCAM, despite dependencies on less-popular rules), and (4) malleability (to enable incremental changes to rule caching as traffic demands change). They propose CacheFlow that supports all these four properties while rewriting, reordering, and caching important switch rules using a novel set of algorithms specifically tailored for the challenges and opportunities in SDN.

3.4.7 Network Function Virtualization

It is widely agreed that network virtualization is the key to the current and future success of cloud computing. As a result, there is a recent trend towards NFV, which essentially transforms existing network devices or physical entities into software-based, virtualized ones. Towards this goal, Martins et al. [80] introduce a high-performance, virtualized software middlebox platform called ClickOS. Each ClickOS VM has only 5MB and can boot in about 30 milliseconds. It is also reported that only 45 microseconds are added and over one hundred of them can be run concurrently to saturate a 10Gb link on a commodity server. By implementing a wide range of middleboxes including firewall, network address translation (NAT), load balance, they show that ClickOS can handle millions of packets in 1 s. Via the concept of NFV, Riggio et al. [81] present an experimental testbed called EmPOWER, which aims at providing an open platform for new networking idea testing. The EmPOWER testbed consists of 30 nodes and is currently used by both undergraduate and graduate students at the University of Trento and by the research staff at CREATE-NET.

Besides data center networks, NFV can be also applied to wireless access networks. Pentikousis et al. [82] argue that carrier networks can benefit from advances in computer science and pertinent technology trends by incorporating a new way of thinking in their current toolbox. They introduce a blueprint for implementing current as well as future network architectures based on an SDN approach. Their proposed architecture enables operators to capitalize on a flow-based forwarding model and fosters a rich environment for innovation inside the mobile network. Their proposal is validated in their wireless network research laboratory. The programmability and flexibility of the architecture are demonstrated.

3.5 Summary

In this chapter, we propose a three-layer cloud networking architecture to fill the gap between application and network for big data processing. Besides the basic architecture, we further discuss many design issues (e.g., language abstraction, big data processing oriented network resource management, performance and efficiency optimization, etc.) that shall be addressed in cloud networking. Some related work on cloud networking and big data, with an emphasis on those which are related to the design issues of cloud networking, are also reviewed and summarized.

References

1. M. Chowdhury, M. Zaharia, J. Ma, M. I. Jordan, and I. Stoica, "Managing data transfers in computer clusters with orchestra," *ACM SIGCOMM Computer Communication Review*, vol. 41, no. 4, pp. 98–109, 2011.
2. M. Hammoud, M. S. Rehman, and M. F. Sakr, "Center-of-gravity reduce task scheduling to lower mapreduce network traffic," in *Cloud Computing (CLOUD), 2012 IEEE 5th International Conference on*. IEEE, 2012, pp. 49–58.
3. B. Heintz, A. Chandra, R. Sitaraman, and J. Weissman, "End-to-end optimization for geo-distributed mapreduce," *Cloud Computing, IEEE Transactions on*, vol. PP, no. 99, pp. 1–1, 2014.
4. W. Yu, Y. Wang, and X. Que, "Design and evaluation of network-levitated merge for hadoop acceleration," *Parallel and Distributed Systems, IEEETransactions on*, vol. 25, no. 3, pp. 602–611, 2014.
5. M. Veiga Neves, C. A. De Rose, K. Katrinis, and H. Franke, "Pythia: Faster bigdata in motion through predictive software-defined network optimization atruntime," in *Parallel and Distributed Processing Symposium, 2014 IEEE28th International*. IEEE, 2014, pp. 82–90.
6. C. E. Hopps, "Analysis of an equal-cost multi-path algorithm," http://tools.ietf.org/html/rfc2992.html, 2000.
7. R. Raghavendra, P. Ranganathan, V. Talwar, Z. Wang, and X. Zhu, "No "Power"Struggles: Coordinated Multi-level Power Management for the Data Center," in *Proceedings of the 13th International Conference on Architectural Support for Programming Languages and Operating Systems (ASPLOS)*. ACM, 2008, pp. 48–59.
8. A. Qureshi, R. Weber, H. Balakrishnan, J. Guttag, and B. Maggs, "Cutting the Electric Bill for Internet-scale Systems," in *Proceedings of the ACM Special Interest Group on Data Communication (SIGCOMM)*. ACM, 2009, pp. 123–134.
9. X. Fan, W.-D. Weber, and L. A. Barroso, "Power Provisioning for A Warehouse-sized Computer," in *Proceedings of the 34th Annual International Symposium on Computer Architecture (ISCA)*. ACM, 2007, pp. 13–23.
10. S. Govindan, A. Sivasubramaniam, and B. Urgaonkar, "Benefits and Limitations of Tapping Into Stored Energy for Datacenters," in *Proceedings of the 38th Annual International Symposium on Computer Architecture (ISCA)*. ACM, 2011, pp. 341–352.
11. R. Urgaonkar, B. Urgaonkar, M. J. Neely, and A. Sivasubramaniam, "Optimal Power Cost Management Using Stored Energy in Data Centers," in *Proceedings of International Conference on Measurement and Modeling of Computer Systems (SIGMETRICS)*. 2011, pp. 221–232.
12. L. Rao, X. Liu, L. Xie, and W. Liu, "Minimizing Electricity Cost: Optimization of Distributed Internet Data Centers in a Multi-Electricity-Market Environment," in *Proceedings of the 29th International Conference on Computer Communications (INFOCOM)*. IEEE, 2010, pp. 1–9.
13. Z. Liu, M. Lin, A. Wierman, S. H. Low, and L. L. Andrew, "Greening Geographical Load Balancing," in *Proceedings of International Conference on Measurement and Modeling of Computer Systems (SIGMETRICS)*. ACM, 2011, pp. 233–244.
14. P. X. Gao, A. R. Curtis, B. Wong, and S. Keshav, "It's Not Easy Being Green," in *Proceedings of the ACM Special Interest Group on Data Communication (SIGCOMM)*. ACM, 2012, pp. 211–222.
15. Z. Liu, Y. Chen, C. Bash, A. Wierman, D. Gmach, Z. Wang, M. Marwah, and C. Hyser, "Renewable and Cooling Aware Workload Management for Sustainable Data Centers," in *Proceedings of International Conference on Measurement and Modeling of Computer Systems (SIGMETRICS)*. ACM, 2012, pp. 175–186.
16. C. Delimitrou and C. Kozyrakis, "Paragon: QoS-aware Scheduling for Heterogeneous Datacenters," in *Proceedings of the 18th International Conference on Architectural Support for Programming Languages and Operating Systems (ASPLOS)*. ACM, 2013, pp. 77–88.

17. L. Liu, H. Wang, X. Liu, X. Jin, W. B. He, Q. B. Wang, and Y. Chen, "GreenCloud: a New Architecture for Green Data Center," in *Proceedings of the 6th International Conference Industry Session on Autonomic Computing and Communications Industry Session (ICAC).* ACM, 2009, pp. 29–38.

18. X. Meng, V. Pappas, and L. Zhang, "Improving the scalability of data center networks with traffic-aware virtual machine placement," in *INFOCOM, 2010 Proceedings IEEE.* IEEE, 2010, pp. 1–9.

19. R. Cohen, L. Lewin-Eytan, J. Naor, and D. Raz, "Almost optimal virtual machine placement for traffic intense data centers," in *INFOCOM, 2013 Proceedings IEEE*, April 2013, pp. 355–359.

20. J. Xu and J. A. Fortes, "Multi-objective virtual machine placement in virtualized data center environments," in *Green Computing and Communications (GreenCom), 2010 IEEE/ACM Int'l Conference on & Int'l Conference on Cyber, Physical and Social Computing (CPSCom).* IEEE, 2010, pp. 179–188.

21. J. Jiang, T. Lan, S. Ha, M. Chen, and M. Chiang, "Joint vm placement and routing for data center traffic engineering," in *INFOCOM, 2012 Proceedings IEEE*, March 2012, pp. 2876–2880.

22. H. H. S. Y. Deze Zeng, Song Guo and V. C. Leung, "Optimal VM Placement in Data Centers with Architectural and Resource Constraints," in *The 15th IEEE International Conference on High Performance Computing and Communications (HPCC 2013),*, 2013.

23. R. Wang, D. Butnariu, J. Rexford *et al.*, "Openflow-based server load balancing gone wild," 2011.

24. M. Sathiamoorthy, M. Asteris, D. Papailiopoulos, A. G. Dimakis, R. Vadali, S. Chen, and D. Borthakur, "Xoring elephants: novel erasure codes for big data," in *Proceedings of the 39th international conference on Very Large Data Bases*, ser. PVLDB'13. VLDB Endowment, 2013, pp. 325–336.

25. S. A. Yazd, S. Venkatesan, and N. Mittal, "Boosting energy efficiency with mirrored data block replication policy and energy scheduler," *SIGOPS Oper. Syst. Rev.*, vol. 47, no. 2, pp. 33–40, 2013.

26. B. Hu, N. Carvalho, L. Laera, and T. Matsutsuka, "Towards big linked data: a large-scale, distributed semantic data storage," in *Proceedings of the 14th International Conference on Information Integration and Web-based Applications & Services*, ser. IIWAS '12. ACM, 2012, pp. 167–176.

27. J. Cohen, B. Dolan, M. Dunlap, J. M. Hellerstein, and C. Welton, "Mad skills: new analysis practices for big data," *Proc. VLDB Endow.*, vol. 2, no. 2, pp. 1481–1492, 2009.

28. R. Kaushik and K. Nahrstedt, "T*: A data-centric cooling energy costs reduction approach for Big Data analytics cloud," in *2012 International Conference for High Performance Computing, Networking, Storage and Analysis (SC)*, 2012, pp. 1–11.

29. F. Chen, M. Kodialam, and T. Lakshman, "Joint scheduling of processing and shuffle phases in mapreduce systems," in *INFOCOM, 2012 Proceedings IEEE*.x IEEE, 2012, pp. 1143–1151.

30. S. Agarwal, J. Dunagan, N. Jain, S. Saroiu, A. Wolman, and H. Bhogan, "Volley: Automated Data Placement for Geo-Distributed Cloud Services," in *The 7th USENIX Symposium on Networked Systems Design and Implementation (NSDI)*, 2010, pp. 17–32.

31. H. Shachnai, G. Tamir, and T. Tamir, "Minimal cost reconfiguration of data placement in a storage area network," *Theoretical Computer Science*, vol. 460, pp. 42–53, 2012.

32. A. Cidon, R. Stutsman, S. Rumble, S. Katti, J. Ousterhout, and M. Rosenblum, "MinCopysets: Derandomizing Replication In Cloud Storage," in *The 10th USENIX Symposium on Networked Systems Design and Implementation (NSDI)*, 2013.

33. H. Jin, T. Cheocherngngarn, D. Levy, A. Smith, D. Pan, J. Liu, and N. Pissinou, "Joint Host-Network Optimization for Energy-Efficient Data Center Networking," in *Proceedings of the 27th International Symposium on Parallel Distributed Processing (IPDPS)*, 2013, pp. 623–634.

34. G. Humphreys, M. Houston, R. Ng, R. Frank, S. Ahern, P. D. Kirchner, and J. T. Klosowski, "Chromium: a stream-processing framework for interactive rendering on clusters," in *ACM Transactions on Graphics (TOG)*, vol. 21, no. 3. ACM, 2002, pp. 693–702.

35. M. Cherniack, H. Balakrishnan, M. Balazinska, D. Carney, U. Cetintemel, Y. Xing, and S. B. Zdonik, "Scalable Distributed Stream Processing." in *CIDR*, vol. 3, 2003, pp. 257–268.
36. L. Tian and K. M. Chandy, "Resource allocation in streaming environments," in *Grid Computing, 7th IEEE/ACM International Conference on*. IEEE, 2006, pp. 270–277.
37. B. He, M. Yang, Z. Guo, R. Chen, B. Su, W. Lin, and L. Zhou, "Comet: batched stream processing for data intensive distributed computing," in *Proceedings of the 1st ACM symposium on Cloud computing*. ACM, 2010, pp. 63–74.
38. H. C. Zhao, C. H. Xia, Z. Liu, and D. Towsley, "A Unified Modeling Framework for Distributed Resource Allocation of General Fork and Join Processing Networks," in *Proceedings of the ACM SIGMETRICS International Conference on Measurement and Modeling of Computer Systems*, ser. SIGMETRICS '10. ACM, 2010, pp. 299–310.
39. G. T. Lakshmanan, Y. Li, and R. Strom, "Placement of Replicated Tasks for Distributed Stream Processing Systems," in *Proceedings of the Fourth ACM International Conference on Distributed Event-Based Systems*, ser. DEBS '10. New York, NY, USA: ACM, 2010, pp. 128–139.
40. "IBM Stream Processing," http://www-03.ibm.com/systems/infrastructure/us/en/technical-breakthroughs/stream-processing.html.
41. "Hortonworks Stream Processing," http://hortonworks.com/labs/storm/.
42. "Amazon Stream Processing," http://aws.amazon.com/blogs/aws/amazon-kinesis-real-time-processing-of-streamed-data/.
43. "Data Torrent," https://www.datatorrent.com/.
44. Z. Zhang, M. Zhang, A. G. Greenberg, Y. C. Hu, R. Mahajan, and B. Christian, "Optimizing Cost and Performance in Online Service Provider Networks." in *Proc. USENIX NSDI*, 2010, pp. 33–48.
45. N. Laoutaris, M. Sirivianos, X. Yang, and P. Rodriguez, "Inter-datacenter Bulk Transfers with Netstitcher," in *Proceedings of the ACM SIGCOMM 2011 Conference*, ser. SIGCOMM '11. ACM, 2011, pp. 74–85.
46. Y. Feng, B. Li, and B. Li, "Postcard: Minimizing costs on inter-datacenter traffic with store-and-forward," in *Proceedings of the 32nd International Conference on Distributed Computing Systems Workshops (ICDCSW)*. IEEE, 2012, pp. 43–50.
47. W. Fang, X. Liang, S. Li, L. Chiaraviglio, and N. Xiong, "VMPlanner: Optimizing virtual machine placement and traffic flow routing to reduce network power costs in cloud data centers," *Computer Networks*, vol. 57, no. 1, pp. 179–196, 2013.
48. G. Lee, N. Tolia, P. Ranganathan, and R. H. Katz, "Topology-aware resource allocation for data-intensive workloads," in *Proceedings of the first ACM asia-pacific workshop on Workshop on systems*. ACM, 2010, pp. 1–6.
49. A. Corradi, M. Fanelli, and L. Foschini, "Vm consolidation: A real case based on openstack cloud," *Future Generation Computer Systems*, vol. 32, pp. 118–127, 2014.
50. A. I. Sundararaj, M. Sanghi, J. R. Lange, and P. A. Dinda, "An optimization problem in adaptive virtual environments," *ACM SIGMETRICS Performance Evaluation Review*, vol. 33, no. 2, pp. 6–8, 2005.
51. J. R. Lange and P. A. Dinda, "Transparent network services via a virtual traffic layer for virtual machines," in *Proceedings of the 16th international symposium on High performance distributed computing*. ACM, 2007, pp. 23–32.
52. N. M. Calcavecchia, O. Biran, E. Hadad, and Y. Moatti, "Vm placement strategies for cloud scenarios," in *Cloud Computing (CLOUD), 2012 IEEE 5th International Conference on*. IEEE, 2012, pp. 852–859.
53. O. Biran, A. Corradi, M. Fanelli, L. Foschini, A. Nus, D. Raz, and E. Silvera, "A stable network-aware vm placement for cloud systems," in *Proceedings of the 2012 12th IEEE/ACM International Symposium on Cluster, Cloud and Grid Computing (ccgrid 2012)*. IEEE, 2012, pp. 498–506.
54. S. Agarwal, M. Kodialam, and T. Lakshman, "Traffic engineering in software defined networks," in *INFOCOM, 2013 Proceedings IEEE*, IEEE, 2013, pp. 2211–2219.

55. "B4: Experience with a Globally-Deployed Software Defined WAN," in *Proc. of ACM SIGCOMM*. ACM, 2013, p. 3–14.

56. C.-Y. Hong, S. Kandula, R. Mahajan, M. Zhang, V. Gill, M. Nanduri, and R. Wattenhofer, "Achieving high utilization with software-driven wan," in *Proceedings of the ACM SIGCOMM 2013 conference on SIGCOMM*. ACM, 2013, pp. 15–26.

57. J. Lee, M. Uddin, J. Tourrilhes, S. Sen, S. Banerjee, M. Arndt, K.-H. Kim, and T. Nadeem, "meSDN: Mobile Extension of SDN," 2014.

58. M. Al-Fares, S. Radhakrishnan, B. Raghavan, N. Huang, and A. Vahdat, "Hedera: Dynamic flow scheduling for data center networks." in *NSDI*, vol. 10, 2010, pp. 19–19.

59. T. Benson, A. Anand, A. Akella, and M. Zhang, "Microte: Fine grained traffic engineering for data centers," in *Proceedings of the Seventh Conference on emerging Networking EXperiments and Technologies*. ACM, 2011, pp.1 8.

60. A. R. Curtis, W. Kim, and P. Yalagandula, "Mahout: Low-overhead datacenter traffic management using end-host-based elephant detection," in *INFOCOM, 2011 Proceedings IEEE*. IEEE, 2011, pp. 1629–1637.

61. X. Wu and X. Yang, "Dard: Distributed adaptive routing for datacenter networks," in *Distributed Computing Systems (ICDCS), 2012 IEEE 32nd International Conference on*. IEEE, 2012, pp. 32–41.

62. G. Wang, T. Ng, and A. Shaikh, "Programming your network at run-time for big data applications," in *Proceedings of the first workshop on Hot topics in software defined networks*. ACM, 2012, pp. 103–108.

63. L. Wang, F. Zhang, J. Arjona Aroca, A. Vasilakos, K. Zheng, C. Hou, D. Li, and Z. Liu, "GreenDCN: A General Framework for Achieving Energy Efficiency in Data Center Networks," *Selected Areas in Communications, IEEE Journal on*, vol. 32, no. 1, pp. 4–15, January 2014.

64. X. Li, J. Wu, S. Tang, and S. Lu, "Let's Stay Together: Towards Traffic Aware Virtual Machine Placement in Data Centers," in *Proc. of the 33rd IEEE International Conference on Computer Communications (INFOCOM)*, 2014.

65. S. Kachele and F. J. Hauck, "Coscanet: virtualized sockets for scalable and flexible paas applications," in *Utility and Cloud Computing (UCC), 2013 IEEE/ACM 6th International Conference on*. IEEE, 2013, pp. 273–277.

66. R. Jain and S. Paul, "Network Virtualization and Software Defined Networking for Cloud Computing: a Survey," *IEEE Communications Magazine*, vol. 51, no. 11, pp. 24–31, 2013.

67. B. Nunes, M. Mendonca, X. Nguyen, K. Obraczka, and T. Turletti, "A Survey of Software-Defined Networking: Past, Present, and Future of Programmable Networks," pp. 1–18, 2014.

68. "Open vSwitch," http://openvswitch.org.

69. "Pantou: Openflow 1.0 for OpenWRT," http://archive.openflow.org/wk/index.php/Pantou_:_OpenFlow_1.0_for_OpenWRT.

70. "POX," http://www.noxrepo.org/pox/about-pox/.

71. A. R. Curtis, J. C. Mogul, J. Tourrilhes, P. Yalagandula, P. Sharma, and S. Banerjee, "Devoflow: Scaling flow management for high-performance networks," in *ACM SIGCOMM Computer Communication Review*, vol. 41, no. 4. ACM, 2011, pp. 254–265.

72. M. Moshref, A. Bhargava, A. Gupta, M. Yu, and R. Govindan, "Flow-level State Transition as a New Switch Primitive for SDN," in *ACM SIGCOMM Workshop on Hot Topics in Software Defined Networking (HotSDN)*, 2014.

73. F. Giroire, J. Moulierac, T. K. Phan *et al.*, "Optimizing rule placement in software-defined networks for energy-aware routing," 2014.

74. X. N. Nguyen, D. Saucez, C. Barakat, and T. Thierry, "Optimizing Rules Placement in OpenFlow Networks: Trading Routing for Better Efficiency," in *ACM SIGCOMM Workshop on Hot Topics in Software Defined Networking (HotSDN 2014)*, 2014.

75. R. Cohen, L. Lewin-Eytan, J. S. Naor, and D. R. Raz, "On the effect of forwarding table size on sdn network utilization," in *Proceedings of IEEE INFOCOM*, 2014.

76. M. Yu, J. Rexford, M. J. Freedman, and J. Wang, "Scalable Flow-based Networking with DIFANE," in *Proceedings of the ACM SIGCOMM 2010 Conference*, ser. SIGCOMM '10. ACM, 2010, pp. 351–362.

77. Y. Kanizo, D. Hay, and I. Keslassy, "Palette: Distributing tables in software-defined networks," in *INFOCOM, 2013 Proceedings IEEE*. IEEE, 2013, pp. 545–549.
78. N. Kang, Z. Liu, J. Rexford, and D. Walker, "Optimizing the one big switch abstraction in software-defined networks," in *Proceedings of the ninth ACM conference on Emerging networking experiments and technologies*. ACM, 2013, pp. 13–24.
79. N. Katta, J. Rexford, and D. Walker, "Infinite cacheflow in software-defined networks," in *ACM SIGCOMM Workshop on Hot Topics in Software Defined Networking (HotSDN)*, 2014.
80. J. Martins, M. Ahmed, C. Raiciu, V. Olteanu, M. Honda, R. Bifulco, and F. Huici, "Clickos and the art of network function virtualization," in *11th USENIX Symposium on Networked Systems Design and Implementation (NSDI 14)*. USENIX Association, 2014, pp. 459–473.
81. R. Riggio, T. Rasheed, and F. Granelli, "Empower: A testbed for network function virtualization research and experimentation," in *Future Networks and Services (SDN4FNS), 2013 IEEE SDN for*. IEEE, 2013, pp. 1–5.
82. K. Pentikousis, Y. Wang, and W. Hu, "Mobileflow: Toward software-defined mobile networks," *Communications Magazine, IEEE*, vol. 51, no. 7, 2013.

Part II
Cost Efficient Big Data Processing in Cloud Networking Enabled Data Centers

Chapter 4
Cost Minimization for Big Data Processing in Geo-Distributed Data Centers

As we have known, cloud networking provides the possibility of orchestrating all resources towards different optimisation goals. For data transferring between the storage units and the processing units in big batch data (e.g., credit billing data) processing, SDN enables the programmers to customize the data routing as needed. Communication cost of large volume data transferring is non-ignorable and shall be carefully addressed in the consideration of cost efficiency. In this chapter, we discuss how to explore communication cost diversity in geo-distributed data centers towards big batch data processing cost efficiency and propose a scheduling algorithm that can be incorporated into the scheduler module in cloud networking [1].

4.1 Motivation and Problem Statement

Data explosion in recent years leads to a rising demand for big data processing in modern data centers that are usually distributed at different geographic regions, e.g., Google's 13 data centers over 8 countries in 4 continents [2]. Big data analysis has shown its great potential in unearthing valuable insights of data to improve decision-making, minimize risk, and develop new products and services. On the other hand, big data has already translated into big price due to its high demand on computation and communication resources [3]. Therefore, it is imperative to study the cost minimization problem for big data processing in geo-distributed data centers.

Many proposals have been made to lower the computation or communication cost of data centers. Data center resizing (DCR) has been proposed to reduce the computation cost by adjusting the number of activated servers via task placement [4]. Based on DCR, some studies have explored the geographical distribution nature of data centers and electricity price heterogeneity to lower the electricity cost [5–8]. Big data service frameworks, e.g., [9], comprise a distributed file system

© Springer International Publishing Switzerland 2015
D. Zeng et al., *Cloud Networking for Big Data*, Wireless Networks,
DOI 10.1007/978-3-319-24720-5_4

underneath, which distributes data chunks and their replicas across the data centers for fine-grained load-balancing and high parallel data access performance. To reduce the communication cost, a few recent studies make efforts to improve data locality by placing jobs on the servers where the input data reside to avoid remote data loading [8, 9].

Although the above solutions have obtained some positive results, they are far from achieving the cost-efficient big data processing because of the following weaknesses:

- The data locality may result in a waste of resources. For example, most computation resource of a server with less popular data may stay idle. The low resource utility further causes more servers to be activated and hence higher operating cost.
- The links in networks vary on the transmission rates and costs according to their unique features [10], e.g., the distances and physical optical fiber facilities between data centers. However, the existing routing strategy among data centers fails to exploit the link diversity of data center networks.Due to the storage and computation capacity constraints, not all tasks can be placed onto the same server, on which their corresponding data reside. It is unavoidable that certain data must be downloaded from a remote server. In this case, routing strategy matters on the transmission cost. As indicated by Jin et al. [11], the transmission cost, e.g., energy, nearly proportional to the number of network link used. The more link used, the higher cost will be incurred. Therefore, it is essential to lower the number of links used while satisfying all the transmission requirements.
- The Quality-of-Service (QoS) of big data tasks has not been considered in existing work. Similar to conventional cloud services, big data applications also exhibit Service-Level-Agreement (SLA) between a service provider and the requesters. To observe SLA, a certain level of QoS, usually in terms of task completion time, shall be guaranteed. The QoS of any cloud computing tasks is first determined by where they are placed and how many computation resources are allocated. Besides, the transmission rate is another influential factor since big data tasks are data-centric and the computation task cannot proceed until the corresponding data are available.

Existing studies, e.g., [4], on general cloud computing tasks mainly focus on the computation capacity constraints, while ignoring the constraints of transmission rate. To conquer above weaknesses, we study the cost minimization problem for big data processing via joint optimization of task assignment, data placement, and routing in geo-distributed data centers. Specifically, we consider the following issues in our joint optimization. Servers are equipped with limited storage and computation resources. Each data chunk has a storage requirement and will be required by big data tasks. The data placement and task assignment are transparent to the data users with guaranteed QoS. Our objective is to optimize the big data placement, task assignment, routing and DCR such that the overall computation and communication cost is minimized.

4.2 System Model

In this section, we introduce the system model. For the convenience of the readers, the major notations used in this paper are listed in Table 4.1.

4.2.1 Network Model

We consider a geo-distributed data center topology as shown in Fig. 4.1, in which all servers of the same data center (DC) are connected to their local switch, while data centers are connected through switches. There are a set I of data centers, and each data center $i \in I$ consists of a set J_i of servers that are connected to a switch $m_i \in M$ with a local transmission cost of C_L. In general, the transmission cost C_R for inter-data center traffic is greater than C_L, i.e., $C_R > C_L$. Without loss of generality, all servers in the network have the same computation resource and storage capacity, both of which are normalized to one unit. We use J to denote the set of all severs, i.e., $J = J_1 \bigcup J_2 \cdots \bigcup J_{|I|}$.

Table 4.1 Notations

Constants	
J_i	The set of servers in data center i
m_i	The switch in data center i
$w^{(u,v)}$	The weight of link (u, v)
ϕ_k	The size of chunk k
λ_k	The task arrival rate for data chunk k
P	The number of data chunk replicas
D	The maximum expected response time
P_j	The power consumption of server j
$\gamma^{(u,v)}$	The transmission rate of link (u, v)
Variables	
x_j	A binary variable indicating if server j is activated or not
y_{jk}	A binary variable indicating if chunk k is placed on server j or not
$z_{jk}^{(u,v)}$	A binary variable indicating if link (u, v) is used for flow for chunk k on server j
λ_{jk}	The request rate for chunk k on server j
θ_{jk}	The CPU usage of chunk k on server j
μ_{jk}	The CPU processing rate of chunk k on server j
$f_{jk}^{(u,v)}$	The flow for chunk k destined to server j through link (u, v)

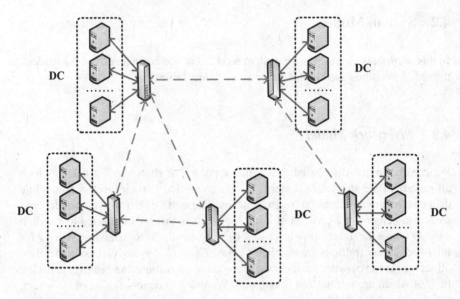

Fig. 4.1 Data center topology

The whole system can be modeled as a directed graph $G = (N, E)$. The vertex set $N = M \bigcup J$ includes the set M of all switches and the set J of all servers, and E is the directional edge set. All servers are connected to, and only to, their local switch via intra-data center links while the switches are connected via inter-data center links determined by their physical connection. The weight of each link $w^{(u,v)}$, representing the corresponding communication cost, can be defined as

$$w^{(u,v)} = \begin{cases} C_R, & \text{if } u, v \in M, \\ C_L, & \text{otherwise.} \end{cases} \qquad (4.1)$$

4.2.2   Task Model

We consider big data tasks targeting on data stored in a distributed file system that is built on geo-distributed data centers. The data are divided into a set K of chunks. Each chunk $k \in K$ has the size of $\phi_k(\phi_k \leq 1)$, which is normalized to the server storage capacity. P-way replica [12] is used in our model. That is, for each chunk, there are exactly P copies stored in the distributed file system for resiliency and fault-tolerance.

It has been widely agreed that the tasks arrival at data centers during a time period can be viewed as a Poisson process [10, 13]. In particular, let λ_k be the average task arrival rate requesting chunk k. Since these tasks will be distributed to servers with a fixed probability, the task arrival in each server can be also regarded as a

Poisson process. We denote the average arrival rate of task for chunk k on server j as $\lambda_{jk}(\lambda_{jk} \leq 1)$. When a task is distributed to a server where its requested data chunk does not reside, it needs to wait for the data chunk to be transferred. Each task should be responded in time D.

Moreover, in practical data center management, many task predication mechanisms based on the historical statistics have been developed and applied to the decision making in data centers [12]. To keep the data center settings up-to-date, data center operators may make adjustment according to the task predication period by period [4, 5, 14]. This approach is also adopted in this paper.

4.3 Problem Formulation

In this section, we first present the constraints of data and task placement, remote data loading, and QoS. Then, we give the complete formulation of the cost minimization problem in a mixed-integer nonlinear programming form.

4.3.1 Constraints of Data and Task Placement

We define a binary variable y_{jk} to denote whether chunk k is placed on server j as follows:

$$y_{jk} = \begin{cases} 1, \text{ if chunk } k \text{ is placed on server } j, \\ 0, \text{ Otherwise.} \end{cases} \tag{4.2}$$

In the distributed file system, we maintain P copies for each chunk $k \in K$, which leads to the following constraint:

$$\sum_{j \in J} y_{jk} = P, \forall k \in K. \tag{4.3}$$

Furthermore, the data stored in each server $j \in J$ cannot exceed its storage capacity, i.e.,

$$\sum_{k \in K} y_{jk} \cdot \phi_k \leq 1, \forall j \in J. \tag{4.4}$$

As for task distribution, the sum rates of task assigned to each server should be equal to the overall rate,

$$\lambda_k = \sum_{j \in J} \lambda_{jk}, \forall k \in K. \tag{4.5}$$

Finally, we define a binary variable x_j to denote whether server j is activated, i.e.,

$$x_j = \begin{cases} 1, \text{ if this server is activated,} \\ 0, \text{ otherwise.} \end{cases} \tag{4.6}$$

A server shall be activated if there are data chunks placed onto it or tasks assigned to it. Therefore, we have

$$\frac{\sum_{k \in K} y_{jk} + \sum_{k \in K} \lambda_{jk}}{K + \sum_{k \in K} \lambda_k} \leq x_j \leq \sum_{k \in K} y_{jk} + A \sum_{k \in K} \lambda_{jk}, \forall j \in J, \tag{4.7}$$

where A is an arbitrarily large number.

4.3.2 Constraints of Data Loading

Note that when a data chunk k is required by a server j, it may cause internal and external data transmissions. This routing procedure can be formulated by a flow model. All the nodes N in graph G, including the servers and switches, can be divided into three categories:

- Source nodes $u(u \in J)$. They are the servers with chunk k stored in it. In this case, the total outlet flows to destination server j for chunk k from all source nodes shall meet the total chunk requirement per time unit as $\lambda_{jk} \cdot \phi_k$.
- Relay nodes $m_i(m_i \in M)$. They receive data flows from source nodes and forward them according to the routing strategy.
- Destination node $j(j \in J)$. When the required chunk is not stored in the destination node, i.e., $y_{jk} = 0$, it must receive the data flows of chunk k at a rate $\lambda_{jk} \cdot \phi_k$.

Let $f_{jk}^{(u,v)}$ denote the flow over the link $(u,v) \in E$ carrying data of chunk $k \in K$ and destined to server $j \in J$. Then, the constraints on the above three categories of nodes can be expressed as follows, respectively.

$$f_{jk}^{(u,v)} \leq y_{uk} \cdot \lambda_k \cdot \phi_k, \forall (u,v) \in E, u,j \in J, k \in K \tag{4.8}$$

$$\sum_{(u,v)\in E} f_{jk}^{(u,v)} - \sum_{(v,w)\in E} f_{jk}^{(v,w)} = 0, \forall v \in M, j \in J, k \in K \tag{4.9}$$

$$\sum_{(u,j)\in E} f_{jk}^{(u,j)} = (1 - y_{jk})\lambda_{jk} \cdot \phi_k, \forall j \in J, k \in K \tag{4.10}$$

Note that a non-zero flow $f_{jk}^{(u,v)}$ emitting from server u only if it keeps a copy of chunk k, i.e., $y_{uk} = 1$, as characterized in (4.8). The flow conservation is maintained

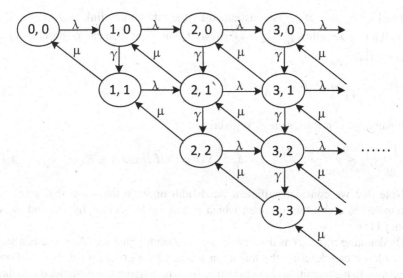

Fig. 4.2 Two-dimensional Markov Chain

on each switch as shown in (4.9). Finally, the destination receives all data $\lambda_k \cdot \phi_k$ from others only when it does not hold a copy of chunk k, i.e., $y_{ik} = 0$. This is guaranteed by (4.10).

4.3.3 Constraints of QoS Satisfaction

Let μ_{jk} and γ_{jk} be the processing rate and loading rate for data chunk k on server j, respectively. The processing procedure then can be described by a two-dimensional Markov chain as Fig. 4.2, where each state (p, q) represents p pending tasks and q available data chunks.

We let θ_{jk} denote the amount of computation resource (e.g., CPU) that chunk k occupies. The processing rate of tasks is proportional to its computation resource usage, i.e.,

$$\mu_{jk} = \alpha_j \cdot \theta_{jk}, \forall j \in J, k \in K, \tag{4.11}$$

where α_j is a constant relying on the speed of server j.

Furthermore, the total computation resource allocated to all chunks on each server j shall not exceed its total computation resource, i.e.,

$$\sum_{k \in K} \theta_{jk} \leq 1, \forall j \in J. \tag{4.12}$$

The loading rate of γ_{jk} is constrained by the rate on any link (u, v) denoted as $\gamma_{(u,v)}$, if a non-zero flow $f_{jk}^{(u,v)}$ goes through it. This condition can be described by a binary variable $z_{jk}^{(u,v)}$ as

$$f_{jk}^{(u,v)} \leq z_{jk}^{(u,v)} \leq A f_{jk}^{(u,v)}, \forall (u, v) \in E, j \in J, k \in K. \tag{4.13}$$

Finally, the constraints on γ_{jk} is given as

$$\gamma_{jk} \leq \gamma^{(u,v)} \cdot z_{jk}^{(u,v)} + 1 - z_{jk}^{(u,v)}, \forall (u, v) \in E, j \in J, k \in K. \tag{4.14}$$

Note that we consider sufficient bandwidth on each link such that $\gamma^{(u,v)}$ can be handled as a constant number, which is mainly determined by I/O and switch latency [14].

By denoting $\pi_{jk}(p, q)$ as the steady state probability that the Markov chain stays at (p, q), we can describe the transition process by a group of ODEs as follows. According to the transition characteristics, the whole figure can be divided into three regions.

Region-I: all states in the first line. In Region-I, except state $(0, 0)$, state $(p, 0)(p > 1)$ transits to two neighboring states $(p + 1, 0)$ and $(p, 1)$. These can be described as:

$$\pi_{jk}'(0, 0) = -\lambda_{jk}\pi_{jk}(0, 0) + \mu_{jk}\pi_{jk}(1, 1), \forall j \in J, k \in K. \tag{4.15}$$

$$\pi_{jk}'(p, 0) = -\lambda_{jk}(\pi_{jk}(p, 0) - \pi_{jk}(p - 1, 0)) \\ + \mu_{jk}\pi_{jk}(p + 1, 1) - \gamma\pi_{jk}(p, 0), \forall j \in J, k \in K. \tag{4.16}$$

Region II: all states in the diagonal line except $(0, 0)$. In this region, all the pending tasks have already obtained their needed data chunk to proceed. Therefore, each state (p, q) in Region-II will transit to $(p - 1, q - 1)$ after processing one data chunk. Then, we have:

$$\pi_{jk}'(p, p) = -\lambda_{jk}\pi_{jk}(p, p) + \mu_{jk}(\pi_{jk}(p + 1, p + 1) - \\ \pi_{jk}(p, p)) + \gamma\pi_{jk}(p, p - 1), \forall j \in J, k \in K. \tag{4.17}$$

Region-III: all remaining states in the central region. Each state (p, q) in Region-III relies on its three neighboring states and also will transit to the other three neighboring states. As shown in Fig. 4.2, the transition relationship can be written as:

$$\pi'_{jk}(p, q) = - \lambda_{jk}(\pi_{jk}(p, q) - \pi_{jk}(p - 1, q - 1))$$
$$+ \mu_{jk}(\pi_{jk}(p + 1, q + 1) - \pi_{jk}(p, q))$$
$$- \gamma(\pi_{jk}(p, q) - \pi_{jk}(p - 1, q - 1)), \quad (4.18)$$
$$\forall j \in J, k \in K.$$

By solving the above ODEs, we can derive the state probability $\pi_{jk}(p, q)$ as:

$$\pi_{jk}(p, q) = \frac{(\lambda_{jk})^p (\mu_{jk})^{B-q} (\gamma_{jk})^{B-p+q}}{\sum_{q=0}^{B} \sum_{p=0}^{B} (\lambda_{jk})^p (\mu_{jk})^{B-q} (\gamma_{jk})^{B-p+q}}, \quad (4.19)$$
$$\forall j \in J, k \in K,$$

where B is the task buffer size on each server. When B goes to infinity, the mean number of tasks for chunk k on server j T_{jk} is

$$T_{jk} = \lim_{B \to \infty} \frac{\sum_{q=0}^{B} \sum_{p=0}^{B} p(\lambda_{jk})^p (\mu_{jk})^{B-q} (\gamma_{jk})^{B-p+q}}{\sum_{q=0}^{B} \sum_{p=0}^{B} (\lambda_{jk})^p (\mu_{jk})^{B-q} (\gamma_{jk})^{B-p+q}}, \quad (4.20)$$
$$\forall j \in J, k \in K.$$

By applying the multivariate l'Hospital's rule, (4.20) can be simplified to

$$T_{jk} = \frac{\lambda_{jk}}{\mu_{jk} \gamma_{jk} - \lambda_{jk}}, \forall j \in J, k \in K. \quad (4.21)$$

According to the Little's law, the expected delay d_{jk} of user requests for chunk k on server j is

$$d_{jk} = \frac{T_{jk}}{\lambda_{jk}} = \frac{1}{\mu_{jk} \gamma_{jk} - \lambda_{jk}}, \forall j \in J, k \in K. \quad (4.22)$$

According to the QoS requirement, i.e., $d_{jk} \leq D$, we have

$$\mu_{jk} \gamma_{jk} - \lambda_{jk} \geq \frac{u_{jk}}{D}, \forall j \in J, k \in K, \quad (4.23)$$

where

$$u_{jk} = \begin{cases} 1, & \text{if } \lambda_{jk} \neq 0, \\ 0, & \text{otherwise.} \end{cases} \quad (4.24)$$

The binary variable of u_{jk} can be described by constraints:

$$\lambda_{jk} \leq u_{jk} \leq A\lambda_{jk}, \forall j \in J, k \in K, \tag{4.25}$$

where A is an arbitrary large number, because of $0 < \lambda_{jk} < 1$ and $u_{jk} \in \{0, 1\}$.

4.3.4 An MINLP Formulation

The total energy cost then can be calculated by summing up the cost on each server across all the geo-distributed data centers and the communication cost, i.e.,

$$C_{\text{total}} = \sum_{j \in J} x_j \cdot P_j + \sum_{j \in J} \sum_{k \in K} \sum_{(u,v) \in E} f_{jk}^{(u,v)} \cdot w^{(u,v)}, \tag{4.26}$$

where P_j is the cost of each activated server j.

Our goal is to minimize the total cost by choosing the best settings of $x_j, y_{jk}, z_{jk}^{(u,v)}, \theta_{jk}, \lambda_{jk}$ and $f_{jk}^{(u,v)}$. By summarizing all constraints discussed above, we can formulate this cost minimization as a mixed-integer nonlinear programming (MINLP) problem as:

MINLP:

min : (4.26),

s.t. : (4.3) − (4.5), (4.7) − (4.14), (4.23), (4.25),

$$x_j, y_{jk}, z_{jk}, u_{jk} \in \{0, 1\}, \forall j \in J, k \in K$$

4.4 Linearization

We observe that the constraints (4.8) and (4.10) are nonlinear due to the products of two variables. To linearize these constraints, we define a new variable δ_{jk} as follows:

$$\delta_{jk} = y_{jk}\lambda_{jk}, \forall j \in J, \forall k \in K, \tag{4.27}$$

which can be equivalently replaced by the following linear constraints:

$$0 \leq \delta_{jk} \leq \lambda_{jk}, \forall j \in J, \forall k \in K, \tag{4.28}$$

$$\lambda_{jk} + y_{jk} - 1 \leq \delta_{jk} \leq y_{jk}, \forall j \in J, \forall k \in K. \tag{4.29}$$

The constraints (4.8) and (4.10) can be written in a linear form as:

$$f_{jk}^{(u,v)} \leq \delta_{uk}\phi_k, \, \forall (u,v) \in E, u, j \in J, k \in K, \tag{4.30}$$

$$\sum_{(u,j) \in E} f_{jk}^{(u,j)} = (\lambda_{jk} - \delta_{jk}) \cdot \phi_k, \, \forall j \in J, k \in K. \tag{4.31}$$

We then consider the remaining nonlinear constraints (4.14) and (4.23) that can be equivalently written as:

$$\gamma^{(u,v)} \mu_{jk} z_{jk}^{(u,v)} + 1 - \mu_{jk} z_{jk}^{(u,v)} - \lambda_{jk} \geq \frac{u_{jk}}{D},$$
$$\forall (u,v) \in E, \forall j \in J, \forall k \in K. \tag{4.32}$$

In a similar way, we define a new variable ϵ_{jk} as:

$$\epsilon_{jk}^{(u,v)} = \mu_{jk} z_{jk}^{(u,v)}, \tag{4.33}$$

such that constraint (4.32) can be written as:

$$\gamma^{(u,v)} \epsilon_{jk}^{(u,v)} + \mu_{jk} - \epsilon_{jk}^{(u,v)} - \lambda_{jk} \geq \frac{u_{jk}}{D},$$
$$\forall (u,v) \in E, \forall j \in J, \forall k \in K. \tag{4.34}$$

The constraint (4.33) can be linearized by:

$$0 \leq \epsilon_{jk}^{(u,v)} \leq \mu_{jk}, \, \forall (u,v) \in E, \forall j \in J, \forall k \in K, \tag{4.35}$$

$$\mu_{jk} + z_{jk}^{(u,v)} - 1 \leq \epsilon_{jk}^{(u,v)} \leq z_{jk}^{(u,v)}, \, \forall j \in J, \forall k \in K. \tag{4.36}$$

Now, we can linearize the **MINLP** problem into a mixed-integer linear programming (**MILP**) as

MILP:

$$\min : (4.26),$$
$$\text{s.t. } : (4.3) - (4.5), (4.7), (4.9), (4.11) - (4.13),$$
$$(4.25), (4.28) - (4.31), (4.34) - (4.36),$$
$$x_j, y_{jk}, z_{jk}, u_{jk} \in \{0, 1\}, \forall j \in J, k \in K.$$

4.5   Performance Evaluation

In this section, we present the performance results of our joint-optimization algorithm ("Joint") using the MILP formulation. We also compare it against a separate optimization scheme algorithm ("Non-joint"), which first finds a minimum number of servers to be activated and the traffic routing scheme using the network flow model as described in Sect. 4.3.2.

In our experiments, we consider $|J| = 3$ data centers, each of which is with the same number of servers. The intra- and inter-data center link communication costs are set as $C_L = 1$ and $C_R = 4$, respectively. The cost P_j on each activated server j is set to 1. The data size, storage requirement, and task arrival rate are all randomly generated. To solve the MILP problem, commercial solver Gurobi [15] is used.

The default settings in our experiments are as follows: each data center with a size 20, the number of data chunks $|K| = 10$, the task arrival rates $\lambda_k \in [0.01, 5]$, $\forall k \in K$, the number of replicas $P = 3$, the data chunk size $\phi_k \in [0.01, 1]$, $\forall k \in K$, and $D = 100$. We investigate how various parameters affect the overall computation, communication and overall cost by varying one parameter in each experiment group.

Figure 4.3 shows the server cost, communication cost, and overall cost under different total server numbers varying from 36 to 60. As shown in Fig. 4.3a, we can see that the server costs always keep constant on any data center size. As observed from Fig. 4.3b, when the total number of servers increases from 36 to 48, the communication costs of both algorithms decrease significantly. This is because more tasks and data chunks can be placed in the same data center when more servers are provided in each data center. Hence, the communication cost is greatly reduced. However, after the number of server reaching 48, the communication costs of both algorithms converge. The reason is that most tasks and their corresponding data chunks can be placed in the same data center, or even in the same server. Further increasing the number of servers will not affect the distributions of tasks or data chunks any more. Similar results are observed in Fig. 4.3c.

Then, we investigate how the task arrival rate affects the cost via varying its value from 29.2 to 43.8. The evaluation results are shown in Fig. 4.4. We first notice that the total cost shows as an increasing function of the task arrival rates in both algorithms. This is because, to process more requests with the guaranteed QoS, more computation resources are needed. This leads to an increasing number of activated servers and hence higher server cost, as shown in Fig. 4.4a. An interesting fact noticed from Fig. 4.4a is that "Joint" algorithm requires sometimes higher server cost than "Non-joint." This is because the first phase of the "Non-joint" algorithm greedily tries to lower the server cost. However, "Joint" algorithm balances the tradeoff between server cost and communication cost such that it incurs much lower communication cost and thus better results on the overall cost, compared to the "Non-joint" algorithm, as shown in Fig. 4.4b and c, respectively.

Figure 4.5 illustrates the cost as a function of the total data chunk size from 8.4 to 19. Larger chunk size leads to activating more servers with increased server cost as shown in Fig. 4.5a. At the same time, more resulting traffic over the links creates

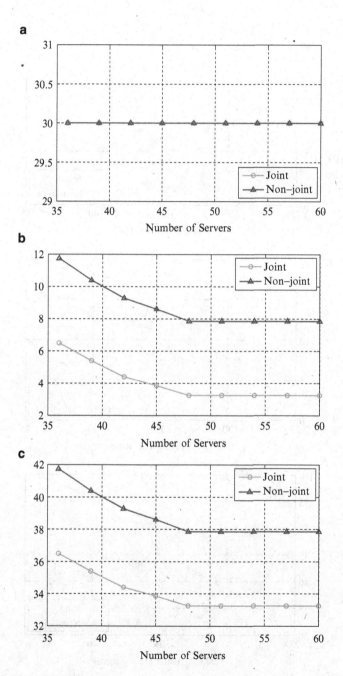

Fig. 4.3 On the effect of the number of servers. (**a**) Server cost. (**b**) Communication cost. (**c**) Overall cost

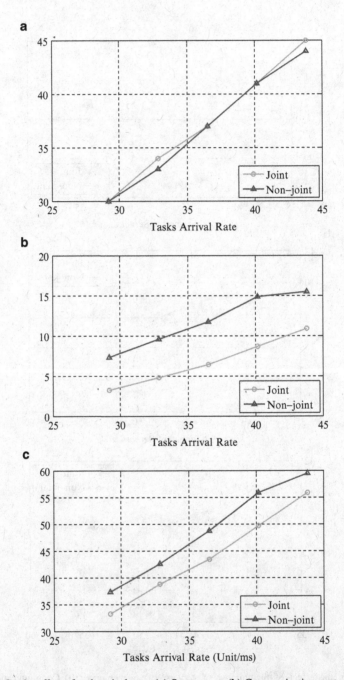

Fig. 4.4 On the effect of task arrival rate. (**a**) Server cost. (**b**) Communication cost. (**c**) Overall cost

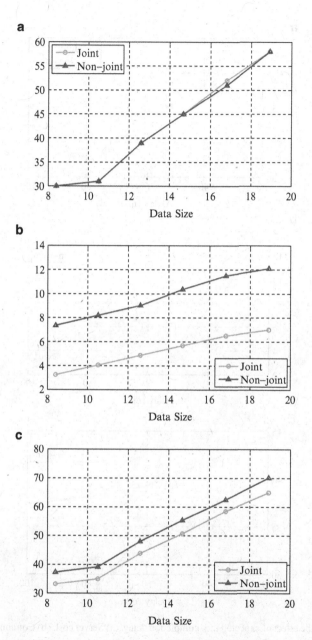

Fig. 4.5 On the effect of data size. (**a**) Server cost. (**b**) Communication cost. (**c**) Overall cost

higher communication cost as shown in Fig. 4.5b. Finally, Fig. 4.5c illustrates the overall cost as an increasing function of the total data size and shows that our proposal outperforms "Non-joint" under all settings.

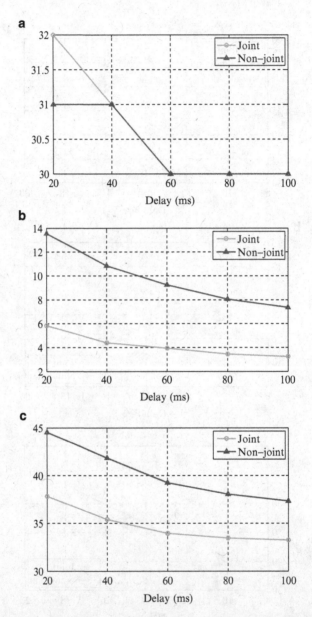

Fig. 4.6 On the effect of expected task completion delay. (**a**) Server cost. (**b**) Communication cost. (**c**) Overall cost

Next we show in Fig. 4.6 the results when the expected maximum response time D increases from 20 to 100. From Fig. 4.6a, we can see that the server cost is a non-increasing function of D. The reason is that when the delay requirement is very small, more servers will be activated to guarantee the QoS. Therefore, the server costs of both algorithms decrease as the delay constraint increases. A looser QoS requirement also helps find cost-efficient routing strategies as illustrated in Fig. 4.6b. Moreover, the advantage of our "Joint" over "Non-joint" can be always observed in Fig. 4.6c.

Finally, Fig. 4.7 investigates the effect of the number of replicas for each data chunk, which is set from 1 to 6. An interesting observation from Fig. 4.7c is that the total cost first decreases and then increases with the increasing number of replicas. Initially, when the replica number increases from 1 to 4, a limited number of activated servers are always enough for task processing, as shown in Fig. 4.7a. Meanwhile, it improves the possibility that task and its required data chunk are placed on the same server. This will reduce the communication cost, as shown in Fig. 4.7b. When the replica number becomes large, no further benefits to communication cost will be obtained while more servers must be activated only for the purpose of providing enough storage resources. In this case, the server and hence the overall costs shall be increased, as shown in Fig. 4.7a and c, respectively.

Our discovery that the optimal number of chunk replicas is equal to 4 under the network setting above is verified one more time by solving the formulation given in Sect. 4.4 that is to minimize the number of replicas with the minimum total cost. Additional results are given under different settings via varying the task arrival rate and chunk size in the ranges of $[0.1, \lambda_U]$ and $[\phi_L, 1.0]$, respectively, where a number of combinations of (λ_U, ϕ_L) are shown in Fig. 4.8. We observe that the optimal number of replica a non-decreasing function of the task arrival rate under the same chunk size while a non-increasing function of the data chunk size under the same task arrival rate.

4.6 Summary

In this chapter, we try to minimize the overall operational cost in large-scale geo-distributed data centers for big data applications by jointly studying the data placement, task assignment, data center resizing and routing. The big data processing is characterized using a two-dimensional Markov chain and the expected completion time in closed-form is derived. This cost minimization problem is then formulated as an MINLP problem. To deal with the high computational complexity, we linearize the MILP problem. Through extensive experiments, we show that our joint-optimization solution has substantial advantage over the approach by two-step separate optimization.

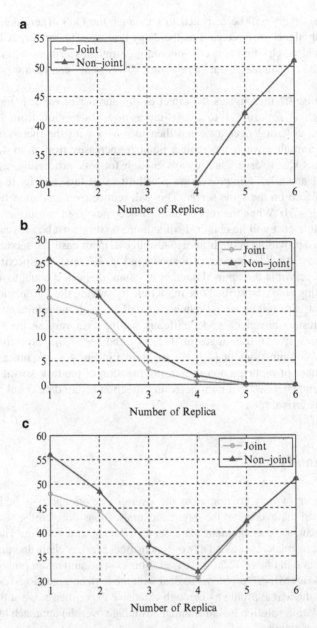

Fig. 4.7 On the effect of the number of replica. (**a**) Server cost. (**b**) Communication cost. (**c**) Overall cost

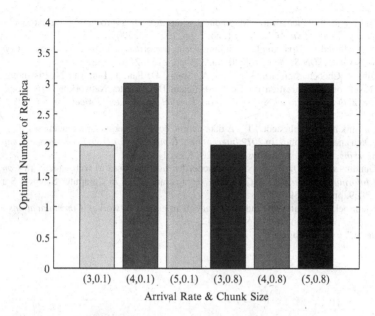

Fig. 4.8 Optimal number of replica

References

1. L. Gu, D. Zeng, P. Li, and S. Guo, "Cost minimization for big data processing in geo-distributed data centers," *Emerging Topics in Computing, IEEE Transactions on*, vol. PP, no. 99, pp. 1–10, 2014.
2. "Data Center Locations," http://www.google.com/about/datacenters/inside/locations/index.html.
3. R. Raghavendra, P. Ranganathan, V. Talwar, Z. Wang, and X. Zhu, "No "Power"Struggles: Coordinated Multi-level Power Management for the Data Center," in *Proceedings of the 13th International Conference on Architectural Support for Programming Languages and Operating Systems (ASPLOS)*. ACM, 2008, pp. 48–59.
4. L. Rao, X. Liu, L. Xie, and W. Liu, "Minimizing Electricity Cost: Optimization of Distributed Internet Data Centers in a Multi-Electricity-Market Environment," in *Proceedings of the 29th International Conference on Computer Communications (INFOCOM)*. IEEE, 2010, pp. 1–9.
5. Z. Liu, M. Lin, A. Wierman, S. H. Low, and L. L. Andrew, "Greening Geographical Load Balancing," in *Proceedings of International Conference on Measurement and Modeling of Computer Systems (SIGMETRICS)*. ACM, 2011, pp. 233–244.
6. R. Urgaonkar, B. Urgaonkar, M. J. Neely, and A. Sivasubramaniam, "Optimal Power Cost Management Using Stored Energy in Data Centers," in *Proceedings of International Conference on Measurement and Modeling of Computer Systems (SIGMETRICS)*. 2011, pp. 221–232.
7. B. L. Hong Xu, Chen Feng, "Temperature Aware Workload Management in Geo-distributed Datacenters," in *Proceedings of International Conference on Measurement and Modeling of Computer Systems (SIGMETRICS)*. ACM, 2013, pp. 33–36.
8. S. A. Yazd, S. Venkatesan, and N. Mittal, "Boosting energy efficiency with mirrored data block replication policy and energy scheduler," *SIGOPS Oper. Syst. Rev.*, vol. 47, no. 2, pp. 33–40, 2013.

9. J. Dean and S. Ghemawat, "Mapreduce: simplified data processing on large clusters," *Communications of the ACM*, vol. 51, no. 1, pp. 107–113, 2008.
10. I. Marshall and C. Roadknight, "Linking cache performance to user behaviour," *Computer Networks and ISDN Systems*, vol. 30, no. 223, pp. 2123–2130, 1998.
11. H. Jin, T. Cheocherngngarn, D. Levy, A. Smith, D. Pan, J. Liu, and N. Pissinou, "Joint Host-Network Optimization for Energy-Efficient Data Center Networking," in *Proceedings of the 27th International Symposium on Parallel Distributed Processing (IPDPS)*, 2013, pp. 623–634.
12. R. Kaushik and K. Nahrstedt, "T*: A data-centric cooling energy costs reduction approach for Big Data analytics cloud," in *2012 International Conference for High Performance Computing, Networking, Storage and Analysis (SC)*, 2012, pp. 1–11.
13. S. Gunduz and M. Ozsu, "A poisson model for user accesses to web pages," in *Computer and Information Sciences - ISCIS 2003*, ser. Lecture Notes in Computer Science. Springer, vol. 2869, pp. 332–339, 2003.
14. L. Kleinrock, "The latency/bandwidth tradeoff in gigabit networks," *Communications Magazine, IEEE*, vol. 30, no. 4, pp. 36–40, 1992.
15. "Gurobi," www.gurobi.com.

Chapter 5
A General Communication Cost Optimization Framework for Big Data Stream Processing in Geo-Distributed Data Centers

For a big data stream processing (BDSP) application, we may have many different processing units in the form of VMs. These VMs are highly correlated by the data streams as one's output may be another one's input. Consequently, the networking shall have a deeper impact to the performance and efficiency of BDSP, compared to batch data processing. Besides, virtualized network functions (VNF), also in the form of VMs, can also be added in stream processing. For example, we may require all the data streams first go through deep packet inspection (DPI) VM before actual processing. How to manage these VMs as well as the communications between them in data centers is critical to the cost-efficiency BDSP. In this chapter, we propose a general communication cost optimization framework and algorithm for BDSP in geo-distributed data centers. The algorithm, which leverages SDN to customize the flow routing, can also be integrated into the Scheduler module [1].

5.1 Motivation and Problem Statement

Big data streams are becoming prevalent at increasing rates, e.g., social media streams, sensor data streams, log streams, stock exchanges streams, etc. Processing and analyzing these data in real-time, i.e., BDSP, has shown its great potential in unearthing valuable insights of data to improve decision-making, minimize risk, develop new products and services. For example, each store of supermarket chains may generate a large number of continuous data covering commodity, sales, customer information, environment information, etc. All these data shall be processed in a real-time manner for efficient supermarket management. In contrast to traditional databases, stream processing systems perform continuous queries and handle data on-the-fly. Much effort from both academia and industries has

D. Zeng et al., *Cloud Networking for Big Data*, Wireless Networks,
DOI 10.1007/978-3-319-24720-5_5

been devoted to BDSP. Several dataflow-based programming architectures, e.g., Twitter's Storm [2, 3] and Spark [4], have been developed to support big data stream processing.

On the other hand, public cloud providers such as Amazon, Google, and Microsoft, have also released various public cloud services supported by large-scale data centers (DCs) to tenants. These DCs are usually distributed at different geographic regions across the globe. For example, Google owns 13 data centers over 8 countries in 4 continents. The rapid development of public cloud has been increasingly attracting individuals and organizations to move their data and services from local to Internet for reliability, security, and expenditure benefits. Modern DCs are virtualization-based and a tenant can rent a handful of virtual resources, e.g., virtual machines (VMs). In the popular approach Infrastructure-as-a-Service (IaaS) cloud model, virtual computing resources can be acquired and released on demand. Public cloud appears to be the perfect infrastructure for realizing the BDSP service, by dynamically adjusting the virtual resources to the current conditions.

With the consideration of ever-growing resource demands of BDSP, it is natural to build BDSP services on the geo-distributed DCs. Big data stream is first characterized by its large data volume. After deploying BDSP onto public cloud, the data explosion will result in a rising of data traffic between DCs. Since most public clouds today rely on Internet Service Providers (ISPs) to connect their geo-distributed DCs, inter-DC traffic is usually significantly more expensive than intra-DC one [5–7]. For example, Amazon's EC2 [8] charges $0.120–0.200/GB for inter-DC transfer across geographic regions, $0.01/GB in the same region, and free-of-charge for intra-DC traffic. Greenberg et al. [9] have revealed that communication costs amount to around 15 % of operational expenditure incurred to a cloud provider. In particular, Chen et al. [10] have pointed out that inter-DC traffic accounts for up to 45 % of the total traffic going through DC egress routers. Undoubtedly, the emergence of BDSP in public cloud will aggravate such situation and make big data equivalent to "big price." It is significant to investigate how to lower the communication cost for BDSP.

Different from conventional stream processing [11, 12] (e.g., queries processing in wireless sensor networks) where each task is attached to a single server (i.e., one-to-one), cloud based BDSP is characterized by that each task can be supported by multiple replicated VMs (i.e., one-to-many) and the locations of VMs are also optional. This provides a new opportunity, but also a challenge, to optimize the BDSP communication cost. If the BDSP VMs are judiciously placed, the communication cost can be potentially minimized. Although VM placement for communication cost minimization has been widely addressed in the literature [13–18], none of them can be applied to BDSP due to the facts that (1) they fail to capture the task semantics in stream processing and (2) most of them are based on an assumption that the number of VMs is fixed and the inter-VM traffic is known.

A typical stream processing task consists a number of inter-dependent intermediate tasks with different join and fork semantics, i.e., synchronous join, asynchronous join, synchronous fork, and asynchronous fork. A unified modelling framework suitable for cloud based BDSP has not been available yet in the literature.

Furthermore, as each task can be supported by a number of replicated VMs, load balancing among these VMs shall be considered without violating the task semantic. In this paper, we are motivated to investigate the communication cost minimization problem with joint consideration of VM placement and load balancing for BDSP in geo-distributed DCs.

To show the limitation of existing studies and illustrate the motivation of our work, we consider a simple example shown in Fig. 5.1, where a BDSP described as a task flow graph in Fig. 5.1a is to be deployed into a public cloud with diverse inter-DC network costs in Fig. 5.1b.

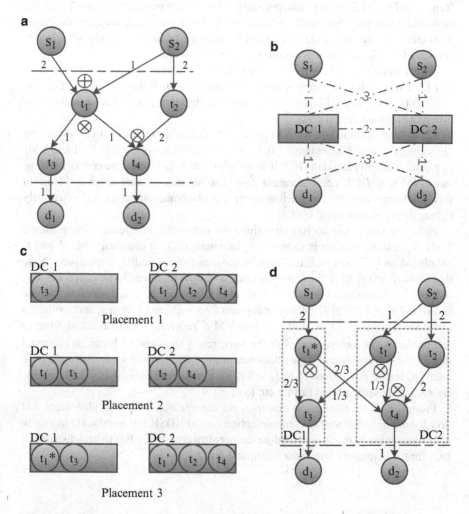

Fig. 5.1 Motivation example. (**a**) Task flow. (**b**) DCs with diverse inter-DC network cost. (**c**) Placement strategies. (**d**) Flow graph for placement 3

As shown in Fig. 5.1a, there are two producers (i.e., s_1 and s_2) as sources, two consumers (i.e., d_1 and d_2) as destinations, and four VMs for four different tasks (i.e., t_1 to t_4) as operators for intermediate processing. To ensure the SLA, certain throughput must be achieved at each consumer. The values on the directed edges denote an example setting of data rates that can ensure the required throughput at each consumer. In BDSP, each task can have multiple replicated VMs with the same processing function.

Two DCs with inter-DC network cost of 2 per data unit are considered, as shown in Fig. 5.1b. Specially, these two DCs are with different network costs between producers and consumers. For example, the cost from s_1 to $DC1$ is 1 while the one from s_1 to $DC2$ is 3. Both producers and consumers are pinned to certain locations. Note that tasks may have different semantics. For example, t_1 requires data flow from either source (indicated by $\oplus$) and its generated data are sent to both t_3 and t_4 (indicated by $\otimes$); t_4 requires data flows from both t_1 and t_2.

We are interested in how to place the task VMs with various semantics into $DC1$ and $DC2$ with balanced flows between the task VMs such that the communication cost can be minimized. Figure 5.1c shows three different placement strategies with different communication costs.

Let us first examine how the VM placement will influence the cost via comparing "Placement 1" and "Placement 2." In Placement 1, VM t_3 is placed in $DC1$ and VMs t_1, t_2, and t_4 are all placed in $DC2$. It is straightforward to get that the cost is 13. If we move VM t_1 to $DC1$, i.e., Placement 2, we can see that the cost drops to 11. From this simple example, we can see that better VM placement strategies will effectively reduce the communication cost.

Next, we show how to further reduce the communication cost using multiple VMs. A feasible solution is shown in "placement 3." Two identical VMs t_1^* and t_1' are placed on $DC1$ and $DC2$ to deal with the data from s_1 and s_2, respectively. Note that VMs t_1^* and t_1' have the same semantic and flow relationship inherited from t_1. In this case, the original task flow graph in Fig. 5.1a can be transformed to the one shown in Fig. 5.1d. VM t_1^* only receives data flow with rate 2 from s_1 and replicates two flows with rate $\frac{2}{3}$ to t_3 and t_4, while VM t_1' receives flow with rate 1 from s_2 and produces two output flow with the same rate $\frac{1}{3}$ to t_3 and t_4. It can be observed that all the semantics and flow relationships are still reserved while there are only inter-DC traffic flows from t_1^* to t_4 and t_1' to t_3 with rates of $\frac{2}{3}$ and $\frac{1}{3}$, respectively. By such means, the cost is further cut to 9.

From the above motivation example, we can see that both VM placement and flow balancing influence the communication cost of BDSP. It is significant to jointly investigate these two issues to explore the network cost diversities in geo-distributed DCs for the communication cost minimization.

5.2 System Model

In this section, we introduce the system model. For the convenience of the readers, the major notations used in this paper are listed in Table 5.1.

5.2.1 Geo-Distributed DCs

The geo-distributed DCs are denoted by a graph $G_d = (V_d, E_d)$ consisting of geo-distributed DC set V_d and their inter-connections E_d. An edge $e_{mn} \in E_d, m, n \in V_d$ is weighted with P_{mn} denoting inter-DC network cost per data unit between DCs m and n. Specially, we assume that intra-DC cost is negligible compared to inter-DC cost and can be viewed as 0, i.e., $P_{mm} = 0, \forall m \in V_d$. A DC $m \in V_d$ is with limited resource capacity R_m.

5.2.2 BDSP Task

5.2.2.1 Task Flow Graph

A BDSP service is modeled by a directed acyclic graph (DAG) $G_t = (V_t, E_t)$, where vertex set V_t includes all the tasks and edge set E_t denotes the data flow links among

Table 5.1 Notations

Constants	
G_t	$G_t = (V_t, E_t)$, the DAG of task flow graph
G_d	$G_d = (V_d, E_d)$, the DC topology graph
P_{mn}	The 1 unit data network cost from DC m to n
A^u	The maximum number of VMs of task u
G_v	$G_v = (V_v, E_v)$, the DAG of VM flow graph
R_i	The resource requirement of VM i
G_e	$G_e = (V_e, E_e)$, the DAG of extended flow graph
s^p	The parent vertexes of $s, s \in V_s$ in G_e
s^c	The child vertexes of $s, s \in V_s$ in G_e
o_{ij}	The output circle vertex, of which the present and the child VMs are i and j
R_m	The maximum resource of DC m
α_{sc}	The scaling factor of flow from s to c in G_e
Variables	
x_i	A binary variable indicating if VM i for task $\eta(i)$ in DC $\delta(i)$ or not
$f_{o_{ij}}$	The data rate of the links connected to $o_{ij}, o_{ij} \in V_c$
f_c	The data rate of the links connected to $c, c \in V_c$

these tasks. The vertices in V_t are classified into three categories, *producer*, *operator*, and *consumer*, according to their roles in the BDSP. Data streams enter the system at the producers and exit at the consumers. A producer $s \in V_t$ generates a type of data with rate F_s. For a consumer $d \in V_t$, certain throughput F_d is required to ensure the SLA. An operator receives "join" flows from its parent tasks and generates "fork" flows to its child tasks. Producers and consumers can be viewed as special operators without join and fork flows, respectively. $e_{uv} \in E_t, u, v \in V_t$ denotes a link with a certain weight going from tasks u to v.

For each operator task $u \in V_t$, at most $A_u (A_u \leq |V_d|)$ replicated VMs are available to be freely placed onto any DCs.

5.2.2.2   Task Semantics

In stream processing, *task semantics* indicate relationships between join flows (i.e., input streams), and fork flows (i.e., output streams), that can be classified in four types "add-join-and-fork," "add-join-or-fork," "or-join-and-fork," and "or-join-or-fork" [19].

As shown in Fig. 5.2, the meanings of symbols $\otimes$ and $\oplus$ on both join and fork flows are summarized as follows.

- And-join ($\otimes$-join): And-join requires data from all join flows simultaneously at some fixed rate. An and-join example is the movie-merging-task that requires synchronized audio and video streams.
- Or-join ($\oplus$-join): Or-join processes data independently from each join flow, not necessarily from both simultaneously. A sampling filter from multiple sources is a typical or-join task.
- And-fork ($\otimes$-fork): And-fork produces multiple fork flows simultaneously with the same stream to each output link. For example, an and-fork task may send a multimedia stream to several different users simultaneously.
- Or-fork ($\oplus$-fork): Or-fork distributes the generated flow over one or multiple output links. Or-fork is common in multi-path routing where packets can be sent to any path link.

Flow constraints are also given in Fig. 5.2 for each semantic type. For example, in Fig. 5.2b, the flow relationship of "and-join-or-fork" described as

$$\alpha_1 f_1 \geq f_3 + f_4$$
$$\alpha_2 f_2 \geq f_3 + f_4,$$

means that the total or-fork flow rate, i.e., $f_3 + f_4$, is upper-bounded by the rate of each and-join flow, i.e., $\alpha_1 f_1$ and $\alpha_2 f_2$, where parameter α_1 and α_2 are the scaling factors describing the expansion/shrinkage relationship between the join flows and fork flows.

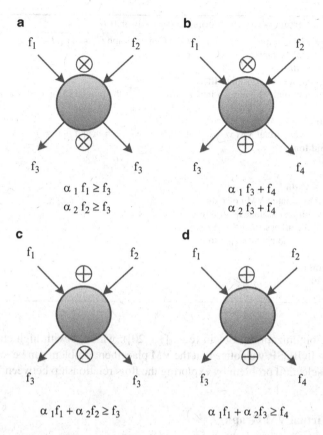

Fig. 5.2 Four types of task semantics. (**a**) And-join-and-fork. (**b**) And-join-or-fork. (**c**) Or-join-and-fork. (**d**) Or-join-or-fork

5.3 Problem Formulation

In this section, we present Virtual VM Graph (VVMG) and Extended VM Graph (EVMG) such that the flow relationships of any task semantic shown in Fig. 5.2 can be described using a unified modeling framework. After that, the communication cost minimization problem is formulated into an MILP problem.

5.3.1 VM Placement Constraints

In BDSP, the streams are actually processed by the VMs of each task. As discussed in Sect. 5.1, VM placement has a deep influence on the communication cost. Traditionally, communication cost aware VM placement is usually formulated as

---

Algorithm 1 Virtual VM graph construction algorithm

Require: Task Flow Graph $G_t = (V_t, E_t)$, Data Center Graph $G_d = (V_d, E_d)$
Ensure: Virtual VM Graph $G_v = (V_v, E_v)$
 1: **for all** $u \in V_t$ **do**
 2:     **if** u is producer or consumer **then**
 3:         add a virtual VM vertex i into V_v where $\delta(i)$ is the pinned DC and $\eta(i) = u$
 4:     **else**
 5:         **for** $m \in V_d$ **do**
 6:             add a virtual VM vertex i into V_v where $\delta(i) = m$ and $\eta(i) = u$
 7:         **end for**
 8:     **end if**
 9: **end for**
10: **for all** $u \in V_t$ **do**
11:     **for all** associated VM i of u **do**
12:         **for all** parent node u^p of u **do**
13:             **for all** associated VM j of u^p **do**
14:                 add an edge e_{ij} into E_v
15:             **end for**
16:         **end for**
17:     **end for**
18: **end for**

---

a quadratic optimization problem (e.g., [18, 20]), which is with high computation complexity. In BDSP, we notice that the VM placement problem can be transformed into a VM selection problem by exploring the flow relationship between VMs.

5.3.1.1   Virtual VM Graph

To tackle this issue, we model and construct the VVMG $G_v = (V_v, E_v)$ as shown in Algorithm 1. Note that, the location of a producer or a consumer is pre-determined. Only one virtual VM vertex in G_v is created for a producer or a consumer (lines 2–3). Recall that each task in BDSP can be supported by multiple replicated VMs with the same processing functions, which can be placed in any DC in the network. In other words, each DC can accommodate a virtual VM for each operator task.

Hence, for each operator task, we create a virtual VM vertex in G_v corresponding to each DC $m \in V_d$ (lines 5–7). The host DC and the corresponding task of a virtual VM $i \in V_v$ are marked as $\delta(i) \in V_d$ and $\eta(i) \in V_t$, respectively. The communication cost per data unit between any two virtual VMs i and j is denoted as $P_{\delta(i)\delta(j)}$, $\forall i$, $j \in V_t$. Based on the task flow, the connectivities among virtual VMs are constructed accordingly, as shown in lines 10–18. An edge $e_{ij} \in E_v, i, j \in V_v$ indicates a possible flow link from virtual VM i to j and is determined by their corresponding tasks.

Each VM's processing semantic is inherited from its corresponding task. Therefore, we construct the connections between virtual VMs according to their corresponding tasks' connections, as shown in lines 10–18. An edge $e_{ij} \in E_v, i, j \in V_v$ indicates a possible flow from virtual VM i to j and is determined by their corresponding tasks.

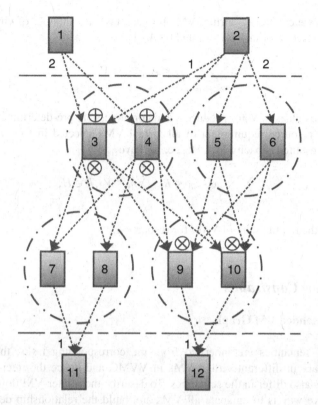

Fig. 5.3 Virtual VM graph for the task flow graph in Fig. 5.1a

Figure 5.3 gives the VVMG constructed base on the task flow graph in Fig. 5.1a and data center graph in Fig. 5.1b. For example, virtual VMs 3 and 4 are constructed for task t_1 in $DC1$ and $DC2$, respectively, i.e., $\delta(3) = DC1, \delta(4) = DC2$ and $\eta(3) = \eta(4) = t_1$.

5.3.1.2 VM Placement Constraints Formulation

To place a VM into a DC is equivalent to selecting one corresponding virtual VM in set V_v. That is, if virtual VM $i \in V_v$ is selected, it means that a VM for task $\eta(i)$ is placed in DC $\delta(i)$. We define a binary variable x_i to denote whether a virtual VM $i \in V_v$ is selected or not as

$$x_i = \begin{cases} 1, & \text{if virtual VM } i \text{ is selected,} \\ 0, & \text{otherwise.} \end{cases}$$

Although we create $|V_d|$ virtual VMs for each task, the number of virtual VMs that can be selected for task u is limited by A_u, i.e.,

$$\sum_{i \in V_v, \eta(i)=u} x_i \leq A_u, \forall u \in V_t. \tag{5.1}$$

Note that, the values of x_i for producers and consumers are pre-determined.

The total resource requirement of all virtual VMs selected in DC m shall not exceed DC resource capacity R_{mh}. Hence, we have

$$\sum_{i \in V_v, \delta(i)=m} x_i \cdot r_{ih} \leq R_{mh}, \forall m \in V_d, h \in H, \tag{5.2}$$

where r_{ih} is the requirement of VM i for resource h.

5.3.2   Flow Constraints

5.3.2.1   Extended VM Graph

As the VM semantics are inherited from the corresponding tasks, the process semantics vary in different virtual VMs in VVMG and hence the inter-VM flow relationships also differ in the semantics. To describe these inter-VM flow relationships, a naive way is to emanate all VMs and build the relationship descriptions with respect to their semantics. Zhao et al. [19] have proposed a unified inter-task flow description framework but it is restricted to the case that each task has only one server (or equivalently VM in BDSP). While in VVMG, there are $|V_d|$ VMs for each operator task, the framework is not applicable for flow description in cloud-based BDSP. To address this issue, We further propose Extended VM Graph (EVMG) $G_e = (V_e, E_e)$ that can be applied to describe the flow relationships for cloud-based BDSP in a uniform manner.

Figure 5.4 illustrates the basic vertex structure in EVMG $G_e = (V_e, E_e)$ for the four types of task semantics in Fig. 5.2. Each EVMG vertex has four layers, i.e., input-layer, producing-layer, distributing-layer, and output-layer. Therefore, V_e can be divided into four subsets, i.e., $V_e = V_i \cup V_p \cup V_d \cup V_o$, denoting the input vertex set, producing vertex set, distributing vertex set, and output vertex set, respectively. In Fig. 5.4, the input and distributing vertices are denoted by squares while the producing and output vertices are by circles. For simplicity, hereafter we call them as square vertex and circle vertex, respectively.

Algorithm 2 briefly summarizes the EVMG construction. Let us first have a look at the basic EVMG vertex construction rules. Each basic EVMG vertex structure is related to one VM in VVMG.

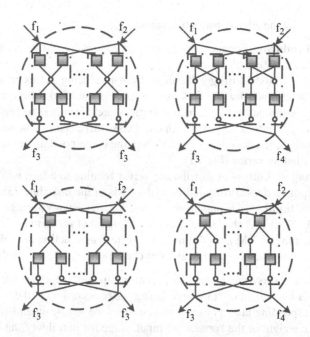

Fig. 5.4 Basic extended vertex structure for four task semantics. (**a**) And-join-and-fork. (**b**) And-join-or-fork. (**c**) Or-join-and-fork. (**d**) Or-join-or-fork

- **Input vertex** The input vertex is determined by the join semantics. For and-join, an input vertex is created for each parent task vertex in task flow graph G_t (line 6), as shown in Fig. 5.4a and b. For or-join, one input vertex is created (line 8), as shown in Fig. 5.4c and d.
- **Producing vertex** The producing vertex is determined by the fork semantics. For and-fork, one producing vertex is created (line 11), as shown in Fig. 5.4a and c. For or-fork, a producing vertex is created for each child task vertex (line 16), as shown in Fig. 5.4b and d.
- **Distributing vertex** The distributing vertex is correlated to the child task, regardless of the task semantics. For each child task, one distributing vertex is created (line 14).
- **Output vertex** The output vertex is determined by the virtual VMs of each child task. Similarly, it is also irrelevant to the task semantics. For each virtual VM of each child task, one output vertex is created (line 22). Specially, we shall see that for each inter-VM connection, there is a corresponding output vertex.

Note that producer and consumer are with only "fork" and "join" semantics, respectively. Therefore, the basic structures for producer and consumer are with three and two layers, respectively. The rest of construction is similar as above.

Next, let us set the edge construction rules:

- **Input → Producing** For each input vertex, an edge is created for each producing vertex (lines 26–30).
- **Producing → Distributing** The edge from producing vertex to distributing vertex is determined by the fork semantics. For and-fork, there is only one producing vertex and all distributing vertices are connected to this producing vertex (line 19). For or-fork, for each child task, there is a producing vertex and a distributing vertex, an edge is created from the corresponding producing vertex to the distributing vertex (line 17).
- **Distributing → Output** A distributing vertex relating to a task is connected to all the output vertices corresponding to the VMs of the task (line 23).
- **Output → Input** Each output vertex refers to an inter-VM edge, e.g., $e_{ij} \in E_v, i, j \in V_v$. Task $\eta(i)$ shall have a corresponding input vertex in the basic EVMG vertex structure for VM j, according to the vertex construction rule. We create an edge connecting each output vertex to its corresponding input vertex (line 34).

In EVMG, to reserve the original flow relationship, each edge is associated with a weight. We set the weight of "input-producing" edge according to the scaling factor α in the corresponding task. For example, consider the "and-join-and-fork" case in Fig. 5.4a. The weight of the "producing-input" edge for join flow f_1 and f_2 shall be set as α_1 and α_2, respectively. For all other edges, their weights are all set as one. Figure 5.5 shows an EVMG example constructed by Algorithm 2 for the VVMG in Fig. 5.3.

Figure 5.5 shows an EVMG example constructed by Algorithm 2 for the VVMG in Fig. 5.3. It can be observed that two producers and two consumers are with three-layer and two-layer structure, respectively, while every virtual VM $i \in V_v$ (dashline box) is translated into a four-layer structure.

5.3.2.2   Flow Constraints Formulation

In EVMG G_e, the flow constraints of all VMs can be represented by the relationships between square vertexes $V_s = V_i \bigcup V_d$ and circle vertexes $V_c = V_p \bigcup V_o$. For each square vertex $s \in V_s$, we denote its parent and child vertex sets as s^p and s^c, respectively, which both include circle vertexes only.

We associate each circle vertex $c \in V_c$ in EVMG with a value f_c to denote the data flow rate. All links connected to circle vertex c share the same flow rate f_c. Note that the flow rates for the producing vertices of consumers are pre-determined according to the required throughputs. The flow rates for the other vertices are variables to be solved. By such means, the flow relationships in EVMG can be uniformly expressed as

$$\sum_{c \in s^p} \alpha_{cs} \cdot f_c \geq \sum_{c \in s^c} \alpha_{sc} \cdot f_c, \forall s \in V_s, \tag{5.3}$$

where α_{cs} and α_{sc} are the weights of edges from c to s and s to c, respectively.

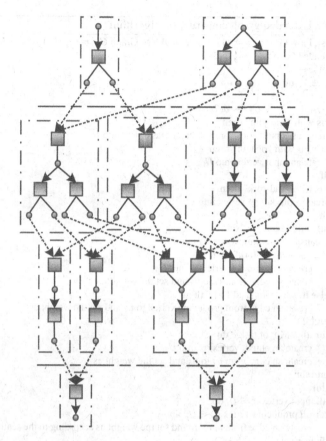

Fig. 5.5 EVMG for VVMG in Fig. 5.3

5.3.3 A Joint MILP Formulation

Whether a virtual VM is selected or not is determined by the corresponding fork flows. For example, if the total fork flow rate of a virtual VM is 0, it shall not be selected; otherwise, it shall be selected. Let $o_{ij} \in V_c$ be the output vertex, of which the present and the child VMs are i and j, respectively. According to the basic vertex construction rules, the rate of a fork flow from VM i to VM j is equivalent to the corresponding output vertex value $f_{o_{ij}}$. The relationship between x_i and the fork flow rate $f_{o_{ij}}$ can be described as

$$\frac{\sum_{j \in V_v} f_{o_{ij}}}{L} \le x_i \le \sum_{j \in V_v} f_{o_{ij}} \cdot L, \tag{5.4}$$

$$\forall i, j \in V_v, o_{ij} \in V_c,$$

Algorithm 2 Extended graph construction algorithm

Require: Task Flow Graph $G_t = (V_t, E_t)$, Virtual VM Graph $G_v = (V_v, E_v)$
Ensure: Extended Graph $G_e = (V_e, E_e)$
1: $V_i \leftarrow \emptyset, V_o \leftarrow \emptyset$
2: **for all** $v_v \in V_v$ **do**
3:      $v_t \leftarrow \eta(v_v), v_t \in V_t$
4:      $U_i \leftarrow \emptyset, U_p \leftarrow \emptyset, U_d \leftarrow \emptyset, U_o \leftarrow \emptyset$
5:      **if** v_v is with "and-join" **then**
6:          create an input vertex for each parent task of v_t into U_i
7:      **else if** v_v is with "or-join" **then**
8:          create an input vertex into U_i
9:      **end if**
10:     **if** v_v is with "and-fork" **then**
11:         create a producing vertex into U_p
12:     **end if**
13:     **for all** child task c of v_t **do**
14:         create a distributing vertex u_d into U_d
15:         **if** v_v is with "or-fork" **then**
16:             create a producing vertex v_t into U_p
17:             create an edge from v_t to u_d and set the weight as 1
18:         **else if** v_v is with "and-fork" **then**
19:             create an edge from producing vertex to u_d and set the weight as 1
20:         **end if**
21:         **for all** VM v of task c **do**
22:             create an output vertex u_o into U_o
23:             create an edge from u_d to u_o and set the weight as 1
24:         **end for**
25:     **end for**
26:     **for all** input vertex $u_i \in U_i$ **do**
27:         **for all** producing vertex $u_p \in U_p$ **do**
28:             create an edge from u_i to u_p and set the weight as according to the scaling factor in the task flow graph
29:         **end for**
30:     **end for**
31:     $V_i \leftarrow V_i \bigcup U_i, V_o \leftarrow V_o \bigcup U_o$
32: **end for**
33: **for all** output vertex v_o in V_o **do**
34:     create an edge from v_o to its corresponding input vertex set the weight as 1
35: **end for**

---

where L is an arbitrary large number. Note that (5.4) can be equivalently expressed using the input vertex values by considering the total join flow rate.

Based on the definition of x_i, we can express the communication cost between any two VMs $i, j \in V_v$ as $f_{o_{ij}} \cdot P_{\delta(i)\delta(j)}, \forall \delta(i), \delta(j) \in V_d, e_{ij} \in E_v$. In the consideration of all above constraints, we can formulate the problem with objective of minimizing the overall communication cost in a form of mixed integer linear programming as:

MILP:

$$\min : \sum_{e_{ij} \in E_v} \sum_{m \in V_d} \sum_{n \in V_d} f_{o_{ij}} \cdot P_{\delta(i)\delta(j)},$$

s.t. : (5.1), (5.2), (5.3) *and* (5.4).

Next we analyze the computational complexity of this formulated problem.

Theorem 1. *The communication cost minimization VM placement problem for BDSP is NP-hard.*

Proof. We consider a special case of the problem that each task is with only one VM, i.e., $A_u = 1$, and all task semantics are "and-join" and "and-fork." In this case, the inter-VM flow values $f_{o_{ij}}, \forall e_{ij} \in E_v$ are predetermined by the producing rates at the producers and the required throughputs at the consumers. We only need to consider how to place the $|V_t|$ VMs onto $|V_d|$ DCs without violating capacity constraints. This is exactly a generalized quadratic assignment problem (GQAP), which has been proved as strongly NP-hard in [21]. ∎

5.4 Algorithm Design

Since it is computationally prohibitive to solve the **MILP** problem to get the optimal solution in large-scale cases, we propose a computation-efficient heuristic algorithm in this section. We observe that the objective function in **MILP** only includes one binary variable x_i. If we relax x_i into a real variable in the range of [0, 1], the **MILP** becomes a linear programming (LP) problem which can be solved in polynomial-time. Therefore, our basic idea is to first solve a relaxed **MILP** problem, and then use the solution to construct a feasible VM placement. Finally, we solve the original **MILP** problem under this VM placement solution, which is essentially an LP problem because all integer variables disappear.

The MILP-based algorithm is presented in Algorithm 3. We first relax all integer variables and solve the resulting LP problem. Note that all the solutions are float values, including the VM placement values $x_i, \forall i \in V_v$. Next, we try to find the VM placement for each task $u \in V_t$. Intuitively, the one with the highest value shall be converted with the highest priority. Therefore, we first sort all $x_i, \forall i \in V_v, \eta(i) = u$ in a decreasing order. The ordered list is denoted as X in line 3. Since task u can have up to A_u VMs, we convert the first A_u elements in X into 1 and the rest as 0 in lines 4 and 5, respectively. After that, we obtain the VM placement solution, i.e., the values of x_i, which are then taken into **MILP**. The resulting problem is an LP with variables $f_{ij}, \forall i, j \in V_v$. We finally solve this LP problem to derive the flow balancing solution in line 7.

Algorithm 3 ILP-based algorithm

1: Relax the integer variables in the MILP, and solve the resulting linear programming
2: **for all** task vertex $u \in V_t$ **do**
3:     Sort $x_i, \forall \eta(i) = u$ decreasingly into set X
4:     $X[k] \leftarrow 1, \forall k = [1, A^u]$, if $X[k] > 0$
5:     $X[k] \leftarrow 0, \forall k = [A^u + 1, |V_d|]$
6: **end for**
7: Take the values of x_is into the MILP, and solve the resulting linear programming

---

Theorem 2. *The LP-based algorithm in Algorithm 3 converges to optimal when* $A_u \to |V_d|, \forall u \in V_t$ *and* $R_m \to \infty$.

Proof. Note that in MILP, the integer variables $x_i, \forall i \in V_v$ are only related to (5.1), (5.2), and (5.4) . There are V_d virtual VMs for task $\eta(i)$. The total number of actually selected VMs shall not exceed $|V_d|$, i.e., $\sum_{i \in V_v, \eta(i)=u} x_i \leq |V_d|$.

When $A_u = |V_d|, \forall u \in V_t$, (5.1) will always be satisfied under all values of x_i. In this case, (5.1) is always satisfied, imposing no constraints on $x_i, \forall i \in V_v$.

When $R_m \to \infty$, (5.2) can be rewritten as

$$\sum_{i \in V_v, \delta(i)=m} x_i \cdot r_i \leq \infty, \forall m \in V_d. \tag{5.5}$$

Obviously, (5.5) is always valid.

For (5.4), without constraints (5.1) and (5.2), x_i can be freely adjusted according to the values of $f_{o_{ij}}$. ∎

From above, we can conclude that when $A^u \to |V_d|, \forall u \in V_t$ and $R_m \to \infty$, all the constraints related to x_i are always satisfied and will not effect the flow variable $f_{o_{ij}}$ as well as the objective in the MILP. As a result, the MILP can be written as

LP:

$$\min : \sum_{e_{ij} \in E_v} \sum_{m \in V_d} \sum_{n \in V_d} f_{o_{ij}} \cdot P_{\delta(i)\delta(j)},$$

s.t. : (5.3),

which is a linear programming (LP) problem itself. Therefore, when $A_u \to |V_d|, \forall u \in V_t$ and $R_m \to \infty$, solving a relaxed MILP in our "MVP" Algorithm 3 is equivalent to solving the LP and optimal solution can be obtained. A DC in the cloud is deployed with hundreds of thousands of servers [22]. Compared with the resource requirement of one VM for BDSP, it can be considered as ∞. The cloud service provider can offer sufficient resource in one DC and a task can have as many VMs as needed in the cloud. In practice, our MVP algorithm provides an optimal-approaching solution.

5.5   Performance Evaluation

In this section, we present the performance results of our MILP-based multiple VM placement algorithm ("**MVP**") by comparing it against the optimal result ("**OPT**") and the traditional single VM algorithm ("**SV**"), i.e., one VM for each task.

In our experiments, we consider a realistic network topology of US NSFNET [23] for our DC network, as shown in Fig. 5.6. Each DC is with the same resource capacity and network cost between two DCs is set according to their shortest path length. For example, the cost between "CA1" and "CA2" is one while the cost between "CA1" and "MI" is two. A DAG generator is implemented to generate random task flow graphs. The locations of producers and consumers, producing rates, required throughput, task semantics, VM resource requirements, etc., are all randomly generated as well. The default settings in our experiments are as follows. The required throughputs are all uniformly distributed within the range of $[0.1, 3]$. All types of resource requirements of VMs for each task are normalized to the DC resource capacity and uniformly distributed within the range of $[0.01, 0.1]$. In each task flow graph, there are 4 producers, 4 consumers, and 30 task operators, each of which is performed by up to 3 VMs. To solve the MILP problem as well as the LP problem involved in the MVP algorithm, commercial solver Gurobi is used. We investigate how our algorithm performs and how various parameters affect the communication cost by varying the settings in each experiment group.

Figure 5.7 firstly shows the communication cost under different maximum number of VMs A_u varying from 1 to 9. We compare the results of the "OPT" and our "MVP" algorithm with 30 and 40 operators, respectively. As observed from Fig. 5.7, the communication cost shows as a decreasing function of the number of VMs A_u when $1 \geq A_u \geq 5$. This is because as A_u increases, more VMs are available for each task, such that the inter-DC traffic can be significantly lowered by flow balancing.

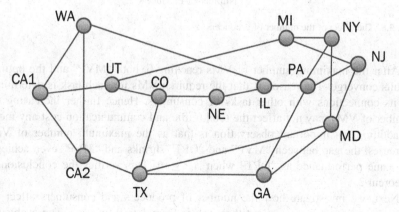

Fig. 5.6 NSFNET

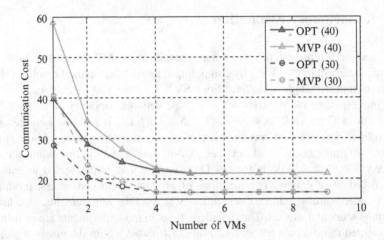

Fig. 5.7 The effect of the number of VM available

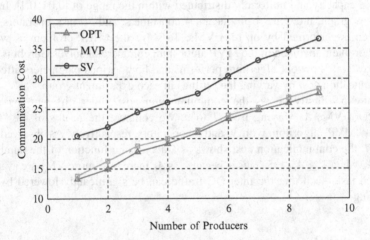

Fig. 5.8 The effect of the number of producers

After the maximum number of VMs reaching 6, both "MVP" and the optimal results converge. The reason is that the required VMs for each task is determined by its connections with other tasks or consumers. Hence further increasing the number of VMs may not affect the total traffic and communication cost any more. In addition, an important observation is that as the maximum number of VMs increases, the gap between "MVP" and "OPT" shrinks and "MVP" even achieves the same performance as "OPT" when $A_u \geq 6$. This verifies the conclusion of Theorem 2.

Next, we investigate how the number of producers and consumers affect the communication cost via varying their values from 1 to 9 for each. The evaluation results are shown in Figs. 5.8 and 5.9, respectively. The advantage of our "MVP"

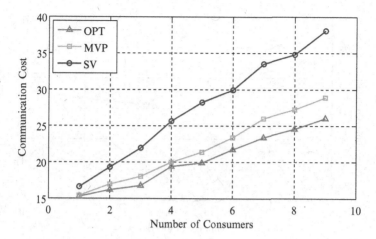

Fig. 5.9 The effect of the number of consumers

algorithm over "SV" can always be observed under any number of producers and consumers. Furthermore, we also notice that the communication cost shows as an increasing function of the number of producers, as shown in Fig. 5.8. This is because, more producers result in more task flows, which potentially increases the inter-DC traffic as well as the communication cost. Similar phenomenon can also be observed in Fig. 5.9 when the number of consumers increases.

Figure 5.10 shows the performances of three algorithms as the number of operators varying from 5 to 30. An interesting observation is that the cost first decreases and then increases with the number of operators. When the number of operators is small, e.g., from 5 to 20, increasing the number of operators provides more optimization space for VM placement and flow balancing. Hence, the results of all three algorithms decrease. However, as the operator number grows, e.g., from 20 to 30, the total flow volume of all operators also increases, even surpassing the benefits mentioned above. This leads to a larger inter-DC traffic, i.e., the communication cost. Under any number of operators, we can always see from Fig. 5.10 that "MVP" outperforms "SV" and performances close to "OPT."

Finally, we study how the three algorithms perform under different required throughputs of consumers, which are all randomly set within the range between 0.1 and a value from 1 to 8 on x-axis of Fig. 5.11. We observe that the communication cost is an increasing function of the throughput. This is because raising the throughputs of consumers will enlarge the task flows over all producers, operators, and consumers, leading to a higher inter-DC traffic and the communication cost. Once more, "MVP" algorithm always outperforms "SVP" significantly.

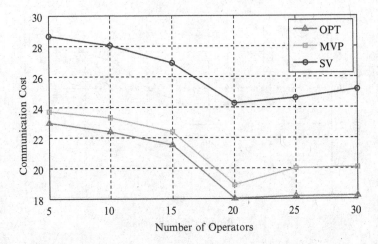

Fig. 5.10 The effect of the number of operators

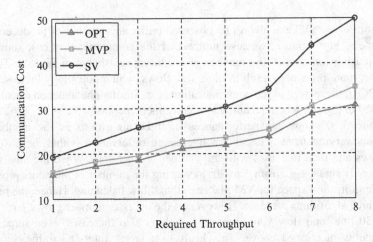

Fig. 5.11 The effect of the required throughput

5.6   Summary

We investigate the communication cost minimization for BDSP in geo-distributed DCs via exploring the inter-DC traffic cost diversities in this chapter. An MILP formulation is proposed to solve this problem, where VM placement and flow balancing are jointly studied. We then propose a low-complexity algorithm based on the MILP formulation. Finally, we show that our "MVP" algorithm performs very close to the optimal solution and significantly outperforms the single-VM based BDSP.

References

1. L. Gu, D. Zeng, S. Guo and I. Stojmenovic, "A general communication cost optimization framework for big data stream processing in geo-distributed data centers," *Online*, 2014.
2. G. Lee, J. Lin, C. Liu, A. Lorek, and D. Ryaboy, "The Unified Logging Infrastructure for Data Analytics at Twitter," *Proc. VLDB Endow.*, vol. 5, no. 12, pp. 1771–1780, 2012.
3. G. Mishne, J. Dalton, Z. Li, A. Sharma, and J. Lin, "Fast data in the era of big data: Twitter's real-time related query suggestion architecture," in *Proceedings of the 2013 international conference on Management of data*. ACM, pp. 1147–1158, 2013.
4. M. Zaharia, M. Chowdhury, T. Das, A. Dave, J. Ma, M. McCauley, M. J. Franklin, S. Shenker, and I. Stoica, "Resilient distributed datasets: A fault-tolerant abstraction for in-memory cluster computing," in *Proceedings of the 9th USENIX conference on Networked Systems Design and Implementation*. USENIX Association, 2012, pp. 2–2.
5. Z. Zhang, M. Zhang, A. G. Greenberg, Y. C. Hu, R. Mahajan, and B. Christian, "Optimizing Cost and Performance in Online Service Provider Networks." in *Proc. USENIX NSDI*, 2010, pp. 33–48.
6. P. Bodík, I. Menache, M. Chowdhury, P. Mani, D. A. Maltz, and I. Stoica, "Surviving failures in bandwidth-constrained datacenters," in *Proceedings of the ACM SIGCOMM 2012 conference on Applications, technologies, architectures, and protocols for computer communication*. ACM, pp. 431–442, 2012.
7. K. yin Chen, Y. Xu, K. Xi, and H. Chao, "Intelligent virtual machine placement for cost efficiency in geo-distributed cloud systems," in *Communications (ICC), 2013 IEEE International Conference on*, pp. 3498–3503, 2013.
8. "Amazon EC2," http://aws.amazon.com/ec2/pricing.
9. A. Greenberg, J. Hamilton, D. A. Maltz, and P. Patel, "The Cost of a Cloud: Research Problems in Data Center Networks," *SIGCOMM Comput. Commun. Rev.*, vol. 39, no. 1, pp. 68–73, Dec. 2008.
10. Y. Chen, S. Jain, V. Adhikari, Z.-L. Zhang, and K. Xu, "A first look at inter-data center traffic characteristics via yahoo! datasets," in *INFOCOM, 2011 Proceedings IEEE*, IEEE, pp. 1620–1628, 2011.
11. M. Cherniack, H. Balakrishnan, M. Balazinska, D. Carney, U. Cetintemel, Y. Xing, and S. B. Zdonik, "Scalable Distributed Stream Processing." in *CIDR*, vol. 3, 2003, pp. 257–268.
12. L. Tian and K. M. Chandy, "Resource allocation in streaming environments," in *Grid Computing, 7th IEEE/ACM International Conference on*. IEEE, 2006, pp. 270–277.
13. J. Jiang, T. Lan, S. Ha, M. Chen, and M. Chiang, "Joint vm placement and routing for data center traffic engineering," in *INFOCOM, 2012 Proceedings IEEE*, March 2012, pp. 2876–2880.
14. K. You, B. Tang, Z. Qian, S. Lu, and D. Chen, "Qos-aware placement of stream processing service," *The Journal of Supercomputing*, vol. 64, no. 3, pp. 919–941, 2013.
15. H. Ballani, K. Jang, T. Karagiannis, C. Kim, D. Gunawardena, and G. O'Shea, "Chatty Tenants and the Cloud Network Sharing Problem," in *Proceedings of the 10th USENIX conference on Networked Systems Design and Implementation*. USENIX Association, 2013, pp. 171–184.
16. W. Fang, X. Liang, S. Li, L. Chiaraviglio, and N. Xiong, "VMPlanner: Optimizing virtual machine placement and traffic flow routing to reduce network power costs in cloud data centers," *Computer Networks*, vol. 57, no. 1, pp. 179–196, 2013.
17. X. Li, J. Wu, S. Tang, and S. Lu, "Let's Stay Together: Towards Traffic Aware Virtual Machine Placement in Data Centers," in *Proc. of the 33rd IEEE International Conference on Computer Communications (INFOCOM)*, 2014.
18. L. Wang, F. Zhang, J. Arjona Aroca, A. Vasilakos, K. Zheng, C. Hou, D. Li, and Z. Liu, "GreenDCN: A General Framework for Achieving Energy Efficiency in Data Center Networks," *Selected Areas in Communications, IEEE Journal on*, vol. 32, no. 1, pp. 4–15, January 2014.

19. H. C. Zhao, C. H. Xia, Z. Liu, and D. Towsley, "A Unified Modeling Framework for Distributed Resource Allocation of General Fork and Join Processing Networks," in *Proceedings of the ACM SIGMETRICS International Conference on Measurement and Modeling of Computer Systems*, ser. SIGMETRICS '10. ACM, 2010, pp. 299–310.

20. K. LaCurts, S. Deng, A. Goyal, and H. Balakrishnan, "Choreo: network-aware task placement for cloud applications," in *Proceedings of the 2013 conference on Internet measurement conference*. ACM, 2013, pp. 191–204.

21. C.-G. Lee and Z. Ma, "The generalized quadratic assignment problem," *Research Rep., Dept., Mechanical Industrial Eng., Univ. Toronto, Canada*, 2004.

22. "Data Center Locations," http://www.google.com/about/datacenters/inside/locations/index.html.

23. B. Chinoy and H.-W. Braun, "The National Science Foundation Network," Technical Report GA-A21029, SDSC, Tech. Rep., 1992.

Chapter 6
Conclusion

Big data is pervasive today and the volume of newly generated data is exploding every day. How to analyze these large data sets (i.e., big data) effectively has become a key issue of business competition, academic research, and industry innovation. The extreme explosion of big data imposes a heavy burden on computation, storage, and networking resources. Cloud, with sufficient resources in large-scale data centers, is widely regarded as an ideal platform for big data processing. How to explore these resources has become the first concern in big data.

Many different big data processing programming frameworks such as MapReduce, Spark, and Storm have been proposed and widely adopted. We have reviewed several representative frameworks for batch data and stream data, respectively. We can see that these frameworks provide convenient ways to explore the bulk cloud resources, especially to the big data processing with high parallelism. However, the underlying networking is still treated as a blackbox and the programmers do not have the privilege to control the network behaviors, besides specifying few parameters. This is because traditional purpose-built networking hardware is not flexible enough to satisfy the dynamic networking demands of big data processing. Fortunately, the newly emerging SDN and NFV technologies enable flexible management of the network by decoupling the controller layer from the underlying hardware. This motivates us to propose cloud networking architecture that is able to manage all resources in a uniform manner. Via cloud networking, different resource scheduling and management algorithms can be specified by the programmers for either performance or efficiency consideration.

Based on the cloud networking framework, we further discuss two case studies on cost-efficiency big data processing. Firstly, we jointly study the data placement, task assignment, data center resizing, and routing to minimize the overall operational cost in large-scale geo-distributed data centers for big data batch applications. We characterize the data processing process using a two-dimensional Markov chain and derive the expected completion time in closed-form, based on which the joint optimization is formulated as an MINLP problem. To tackle the high computational

© Springer International Publishing Switzerland 2015
D. Zeng et al., *Cloud Networking for Big Data*, Wireless Networks,
DOI 10.1007/978-3-319-24720-5_6

complexity of solving our MINLP, we linearize it into an MILP problem. In the second case study, we investigate the communication cost minimization for BDSP in geo-distributed data centers via exploring the inter-DC traffic cost diversity. VM placement and flow balancing are jointly considered. For computation efficiency, we propose VVMG and transform the VM placement problem into a VM selection problem. We then further invent EVMG that enables uniform description of the flow relationships for different subtask semantics. An MILP formulation is built for the communication cost problem. To tackle the high computational complexity of solving MILP, we then propose "MVP" algorithm by relaxing the MILP formulation. Both algorithms can be incorporated into the Scheduler module in cloud networking. We also have evaluated the efficiency of our proposals via extensive simulations.

Printed in the United States
By Bookmasters